Justice Delayed
The Catherine Janet Walsh Story

by

Steve Hallock

For information, please address:
The Artists' Orchard, LLC
P.O. Box 113593
Pittsburgh, PA 15241

www.theartistsorchard.com

ISBN: 978-0-9964592-0-4

Produced in the United States of America

For Rebecca

In memory of Peter Caltury,
who epitomized a father's love
and a father's anguish

The man who lies to himself and listens to his own lie comes to such a pass that he cannot distinguish the truth within him, or around him, and so loses all respect for himself and for others. And having no respect he ceases to love, and in order to occupy and distract himself without love he gives way to passions and coarse pleasures, and sinks to bestiality in his vices, all from continual lying to other men and to himself.

—Fyodor Dostoyevsky, "The Brothers Karamazov"

A good whodunit makes a good book or movie, but it is frustrating to live.

—Andrew Gall, assistant chief of detectives for the Beaver County District Attorney's Office

Introduction

On September 3, 2014, the Reuters wire service reported the freeing of two North Carolina men after more than three decades of incarceration for the rape and murder of an 11-year-old girl – a crime that they did not commit. According to the report, 50-year-old Henry McCollum and his 46-year-old half brother, Leon Brown, had been charged and convicted of killing Sabrina Buie and leaving her body in a field near the small town of Red Springs, North Carolina. McCollum had been sentenced to death and was the state's longest-serving death row inmate. Brown's sentence had been reduced to life following a second trial.

The men signed a "detailed" confession, but they later said they had been "coerced to do so with promises of release during intense interrogations. Court records show that both men are intellectually disabled, with limited abilities to read or write," Reuters reported.

This good news for McCollum and Brown relates to the subject matter of the book at hand by two factors: the use of DNA analysis in solving crimes, and the extreme length of time involved to resolve a violent crime. In both the exoneration of wrongly convicted men in the case of McCollum and Brown, and the closure of the murder case of a young woman slain more than three decades ago in a small, industrial Southwestern Pennsylvania community nestled in the foothills along the Ohio River, justice prevailed decades after the murders.

***

The story of the Catherine Janet Walsh murder is actually several stories. It is the tale of a tenacious young police detective in the town of Monaca, Pennsylvania, who was the first responding officer to the call from Janet's father. He discovered his daughter's body in her bedroom after she failed to show up for work one Saturday morning that Labor Day weekend in 1979. This officer promised justice to Janet's father and remained on the case for more than 30 years.

It is the story of a heinous crime in a small, close community whose residents know each other and hang out together at the diners, barber shops and beauty salons, in the parks and bars. Its people work together in what once was a multi-community metroplex of steel mills and factories replaced by shops and service industries, still a blue-collar, hard-working population. It is a community where violent crime has always been rare, where the shock of the murder of this young secretary estranged from her husband and high school sweetheart reverberated up and down the main streets and side avenues of these small towns hugging the Ohio River.

It is the story of family and friends first devastated by and then coping with an inexplicable crime with few clues and many suspects, each of whom knew the victim and at least a couple of whom had possible motive. And of a case that went cold, though never was closed, for nearly three decades because of the lack of evidence strong enough to lead to an arrest, let alone a conviction.

It is the story of forensic science, like the DNA evidence that cleared McCollum and Brown in North Carolina, that led to the conviction of a man who knew Janet Walsh intimately and who took advantage of that intimacy to gain entry to her home in the early morning hours of the Saturday before Labor Day to strangle her – leaving behind seminal stains that, though undetected then, would remain sealed in evidence envelopes to be brought into a Beaver County courtroom nearly 34 years later to convince a jury that the man who had claimed Janet as his lover had killed her.

And once a suspect was apprehended due to DNA technology, it became a story of a courtroom drama in which two assistant district attorneys battled a defense lawyer, who would become a judge after this, his final case, using not only contradicting expertise in the science of DNA but dueling character witnesses and an alibi that appeared, at first, to clear the man incriminated by the DNA evidence.

Finally, the answer for those who question why the events of three-and-a-half decades ago should still interest us today, it is a narrative containing the elements that have made Greek tragedy and the plays of the likes of Shakespeare and O'Neill pertinent to modern spectators of the human drama. Friendship, solitude, the seeking of happiness, the longing for companionship, the pursuit of truth in the nooks and shadows of betrayal and deceit, foul murder, familial love – these are the timeless rudiments of the mortal condition all played out in a small-town murder on the banks of an old and wandering river.

Because of the technological and scientific methods used in the Walsh investigation, along with the methods of the police that mirrored tactics of other investigations involving DNA forensics, it is necessary in this book to trace, with some detail, the evolution of that forensic science, from its first use to convict a British man of two brutal murders in the 1980s to the technological advances such as special lighting to detect decades-old semen stains on bed sheets in the new century. The science of this case is a key element – indeed, almost a character of the story – of what remained for so long a mystery involving five primary suspects. The science played a major role in this case, along with the human element of a police detective who would not let the murder of Janet Walsh remain a cold case forever.

***

I had immense help in piecing together this story from that detective, Andrew Gall, now with the Beaver County District Attorney's Office. Detective Gall allowed me full access to the case file of the Janet Walsh murder investigation, which included initial police reports and interviews with the suspects, neighbors, friends and relatives of the victim. He also gave considerable time to this writing project, along with a tour of the neighborhoods and the murder scene. Other sources used for this book included the full transcript of the murder trial, newspaper accounts of the murder and of the ensuing investigation and trial, newspaper and magazine articles, research journals, and books used for historical documentation of the development and evolution of DNA forensics, and interviews with trial jurors and case participants.

I owe a thank-you to Detective Gall, without whom this book would not have been possible, to his boss, Beaver County District Attorney Anthony Berosh, to Assistant District Attorneys Frank Martocci and Brittany Smith, and to jurors who provided valuable insight into the reasoning behind their verdict, but, at their request, remain unnamed in this book.

I also want to thank my publisher and editor, Sherry Linger Kaier, for her meticulous eye for detail and for her encouragement in the process of producing this book.

1

Andrew Gall had seen corpses and blood during his early days as a Monaca police officer. But not like this. He'd experienced dead bodies from automobile fatalities. But not like this. Those experiences hadn't prepared him for the scene he found at the small one-bedroom apartment in Southwestern Pennsylvania's Lower Monaca that Labor Day weekend Saturday afternoon in 1979.

It was an eerie sight: the body of a young woman lying on her stomach, her hands bound by a robe tie behind her, nude from the waist down with a nightgown covering her upper body. A scarf or bandana bound her neck; she'd been strangled with no sign of a struggle, no indication of anything missing, no sign of disarray. All was neat and tidy in the apartment, except for the body of 23-year-old Catherine Janet Walsh –

known in the community and to friends as Janet.

The next morning's Beaver County Times told the story of what Gall found after being summoned by an emergency phone call from the victim's father who, along with his wife, had discovered their daughter's body in her bedroom after she had failed to show up for work that morning.

"The quiet residential neighborhood of Indiana Avenue, Monaca, is stunned and in mournful silence," began the story by reporter Jack Simon beneath a headline that read: "Woman slain by strangler," accompanied by a black-and-white photo of Walsh, her dark hair cropped short just over her ears, wearing a white turtleneck sweater. "One of its residents, an attractive blue-eyed brunette who worked as a secretary in the community is dead – the victim of a strangler who remains at large."

The story reported that Walsh was discovered in her bedroom shortly after noon on September 1 by her parents on the first floor of the two-story frame duplex at 935 Indiana Ave.

"She was pronounced dead at 1:05 p.m. by Harper J. Simpson, deputy county coroner, who said an autopsy confirmed that death was the result of strangulation," the report continued. "He said there was no indication of rape. Catherine, separated from her husband since May, was described as a quiet person of good character and well-liked by those who knew her. She was employed at Reliable Refrigeration Co., Monaca, and won sewing contests, sponsored by Junior Woman's Clubs of Western Pennsylvania, in 1973 and 1974."

The story described a neighborhood in shock.

"There was a hush over Indiana Avenue last evening. Barricades at Ninth and 10th streets sealed off the scene of the crime from onlookers. A few residents sat on front porches looking at the two-story yellow and brown home in which Catherine resided. The sidewalks were free of pedestrians.

"On the porch of Catherine's apartment were two green lawn chairs where neighbors said she often sat with a friend to chat. The lawn around the home was well-groomed. Her apartment indoors was moderately furnished but comfortable. It had been carefully scrutinized during the day by investigators in search of clues. Now it was quiet with all locks secured. Parked in front of the home was Catherine's green Monte Carlo with white vinyl top. Across the street is Chris Mangia Elementary School. And behind the home is the Batchelor Funeral Home, where Catherine will lie in rest today and Monday.

" 'Why would someone take the life of such a nice young woman?' asked one of Catherine's neighbors."

That was the precise question that law enforcement officials were asking as they tried to figure out the motive of the grisly murder scene they discovered at the apartment – details of which they had not shared with the journalists covering the murder.

The first officer on the scene was the 25-year-old Gall, who was driving on patrol on Old Brodhead Road that Saturday when he got the call at 12:19 p.m. from dispatch to report to Walsh's apartment. The case would be his first homicide investigation.

"I went up to the front door of the house

and knocked at the door," Gall would recall more than 30 years later. Walsh's father, Peter Caltury, who had called the police, opened the front door. "He let me in. His wife, Mary Jane, was in that first part of the room. It's kind of like a sun porch."

The father, Gall said, "indicated that his daughter was in the bedroom, and he thought she was dead. I went straight back to the bedroom and viewed the body."

Walsh was beneath a sheet in her bed, face down. The sheet, Gall said, "was up near her neck, and I looked at her face. By the way the face looked, you knew she was dead." Gall described finding a light blue workman's handkerchief around her neck, which had been used to strangle her and was tied "very tightly, and it was knotted right up here under her hair." She wore a nightgown, which had been pulled up to reveal her body, nude from the waist down. Her hands were bound behind her back by a white cord. Her father, who had arrived at the apartment that morning, was the first to view the murder scene. He had called his daughter's work looking for her to inquire about a bank deposit he would be making for her. But she was not at work, and her boss, Ronald Ciccozzi, said he was looking for her too.

Caltury went to the apartment, rang the front bell and knocked on the door, then tried the back door and tapped on the bedroom window. Then he went home, where his wife told him that someone had called over concern about Walsh "because," he told police, "it's not like her not to call in or whatever, if she's not going to be there."

Walsh's mother had already called Walsh's former neighbor and friend, Margie Farinacci, who said she didn't know Walsh's whereabouts, and the phone line of Walsh's closest friend, Barbara Cinderich, was busy.

"So that's when I got scared," Caltury told police that Saturday. He grabbed a set of keys he had to Walsh's apartment. "I wanted to come down myself and my wife, she insisted she wanted to come along too 'cause she was getting a little apprehensive. So I parked in the yard in back. Went in the back door and called, no answer, and I looked through the bedroom door and I saw, you know, it just looked like a bubble to me then, and went in and called her and called and then when I saw it was her, you know, her hair, and she was face down, shook her and pulled the sheet down a little bit, and then when I saw that, she was sleeping kind of funny, if she was sleeping, and I pulled the rest of the way, and her arms were tied with a white rope or whatever, and I tried to get a pulse, you know, nothing. And then that's when I called you people."

Potential suspects arose as Gall and others – including Monaca Police Department Chief Lawrence R. Conti, state patrol officers and the Beaver County Major Crime Task Force led by Bernard Cashdollar – continued their interview of Walsh's father. Asked about the possibility of problems between Walsh and her estranged husband, Scott Walsh, Caltury responded that his daughter "was a little irritated with the way he was carrying on, you know, and she decided to leave him. That's all."

What did Caltury mean by "irritated?"

"Well, I guess, he was going ice skating and she got sick one time and he didn't take care of her like she thought he should have, little things I guess ..."

Caltury told police he had seen Scott Walsh just that morning driving by Janet's house. Scott, who was returning from running errands and a stop at the post office, told him he had dropped off at Janet's apartment a support check and set of keys he had found, which had a Reliable Refrigeration tag attached. He had shoved them in her mail slot, he told his father-in-law. Caltury said his daughter had asked him to change her door locks, but he had not gotten around to it. Caltury said that besides telephoning the police, he also had called his two sons and his brother-in-law, Leo Bianco, who took care of rental properties. He then mentioned one other name to police: Scott Hopkins.

"I don't know how many times he was down there, if he was ever there," Caltury said of Hopkins. But, he said, Janet's friend Barbara Cinderich, who had stayed with Janet while waiting for an apartment to be ready to move into, had mentioned Hopkins, "and I guess he called pretty late at night or early in the morning. She says that one night, early in the morning, that she (Janet) didn't want anything to do with him and ... stop bothering her."

Caltury said that Cinderich had told Scott Walsh about Hopkins, and when Caltury talked to Scott Walsh on the phone later that day about Hopkins, "he was pretty bitter about that time. Well, it's what he said to me. 'Now,' he said, 'I'm really bitter' … Evidently, this fellow was running around with Margie … And Janet was along one time … with Margie and then he was talking to Janet. Maybe that's how … I don't know."

That was pretty much the sentiment of all involved in the initial investigation into the murder of Janet, who had followed the custom of many folks in this small community on the Ohio River of going by their middle name in familiar usage instead of their first. The Beaver County Times reported in a front-page follow-up story published September 5 that clues were "sketchy," though reporters had evidently learned more about the case – including the estimated time of death and negative results of a rape kit.

"Police are continuing to work around-the-clock in hopes of uncovering a clue that will lead them to the person who murdered Catherine

Walsh of Monaca," said the report. "The attractive 23-year-old woman was found by her parents Saturday morning strangled to death in the bedroom of her apartment.

"Mrs. Walsh, who authorities said was at a local disco and restaurant Friday evening, was discovered the following morning with one of her scarves tied around her neck. Her hands were tied behind her and she was partially clothed.

"Mrs. Walsh, who was separated from her husband Scott, was not sexually molested, and authorities are hard-pressed to find a motive for the murder. According to one source, the actual murder occurred between 3:30 and 4 a.m. There were no signs of forced entry to the victim's apartment and nothing is believed missing. A small amount of money was still lying on the table."

Neighbors also were clueless.

"From all reports, none of the neighbors who live near the apartment on Indiana Avenue heard any disturbance that morning. Investigating officers indicated there was no sign of a struggle in the bedroom."

The story concluded: "While police have

no prime suspects in the case, they have not ruled out the possibility that the murderer was a woman. Mrs. Walsh was buried yesterday."

On September 16, the newspaper reported that the county district attorney had entered the investigation in the wake of rumors circulating through the community and the release of a composite sketch of a man believed to be connected to the case.

District Attorney Edward J. Tocci, who had scheduled a meeting with state, county and Monaca investigators to discuss the case, "expressed concern about the lack of official information released about the investigation, especially the composite of a man wanted for questioning which was compiled by a county detective shortly after the slaying," the newspaper reported. "A rumor that a woman, mentioned by name, was arrested spread through the county last week," the report continued. " 'We must put an end to all these silly rumors which are affecting people's reputations,' the district attorney explained."

The composite sketch was of a "young, clean-shaven man wearing metal frame glasses who asked a neighbor about 9 p.m. Sept. 1 for directions to Catherine's residence," the report said, adding that state police said the man was "only wanted for questioning."

Bernard Cashdollar, coordinator of the county Major Crime Task Force, told the newspaper that more than 100 people had been interviewed during the investigation but that, "this is a very unusual case in that police have not received a single phone tip."

Cashdollar "assured that there is no new development in the case. 'We're trying to work quietly and in good judgment and we really don't have anything further to release at this time,' he said."

Meanwhile, as the residents of Monaca and its neighboring Ohio River communities pondered why this unknown assailant had murdered an innocent young woman, investigating officers were busy questioning anybody and everybody who knew Janet Walsh to piece together her story, beginning with the events of the day and evening prior to the early morning murder.

That Friday night in 1979 offered a plethora of entertainment possibilities for a young secretary in the midst of divorcing her high school sweetheart. One option was to stay in and watch TV in the tidy, four-room apartment that she rented from her grandmother in Beaver County's Lower Monaca, an industrial – primarily steel mill – town at the junction of the Beaver and Ohio Rivers. The television beckoned with sitcoms and crime. Roger and Tony were switching bodies on "I Dream of Jeannie," and in Mayberry, Deputy Barney Fife would resign because he feared Sheriff Andy Taylor was trying to ease him out of his job. In the world of drama, a gang of unsavory gamblers planned to scam attendees of a farm-equipment convention until "Dragnet's" Friday and Gannon came along to thwart the plot; James Rockford helped out a prostitute friend, played by Rita Moreno, after she witnessed a gangland murder. For those more interested in serious fare, William Buckley's guests on "Firing Line" were radio and television commentator Dorothy Fuldhem and Ben Stein, author of "The View From Sunset Boulevard."

On the big screen, Andy Warhol's "Frankenstein" was at the Kane Road Drive-In Theatre in Aliquippa, along with Allen Funt's "Candid Camera" film spinoff, "What Do You Say To A Naked Lady?" The ABC Drive-In offered "Star Wars" and "Planet of the Apes." At the Cinema, Robin Williams was making his film debut in "Can I Do It Til I Need Glasses?" For those interested in higher culture, The Red Barn Theatre was staging Neil Simon's comedy "God's Favorite," directed by Mary Jane Tillia, according to The Beaver County Times entertainment listings for the weekend.

But no. Janet and her former neighbor Margie Farinacci, of Upper Monaca – the neighborhood of homes in the heights up on the bluff that overlooked Lower Monaca, downtown and the rivers – had decided to meet up for drinks. That choice, too, offered numerous options in the small, closely-knit metroplex of 40,000 or 50,000 folks who worked in the mills and factories and lived in a gathering of towns hunkered among the rolling hills and bluffs along the Ohio that included not only Monaca, but Center Township, Bridgewater, Ambridge, Rochester, East Rochester, Economy, Aliquippa, New Brighton, Baden, Beaver Falls and Beaver – the county seat, which was a dry town whose residents had to drive elsewhere to slake their alcohol thirst. Plenty of bar stools, some of them offering a view of live entertainment and all within a 10- to 15-minute drive of each other, awaited the Labor Day weekend crowd on this Friday night.

The Rocco Sisters were performing at the Top of the Mall in the Beaver County Mall. Down the road, Sal Angel Plus 2 were holding court at the El Morocco Lounge, Papa Pags was at the Hide-A-Way Inn, and Fez offered the sounds of 4 Shades in Aliquippa. In New Brighton, Inside Track was in the cozy Serafino Lounge at Serafino's Rusty Nail, and Scrimshaw was presenting "Our Own Jerry Dattilo."

But this was the '70s, and disco was still king at the end of the decade. K.T. was spinning disco and oldies at Armando's in Rochester; Jersey's Restaurant in Rochester had the "Greatest in Disco & Golden Oldies" from 10 to 2. Janet and Margie decided to meet for drinks at the Top of the Mall to celebrate Janet's impending divorce and then to meet a couple of friends and check out the grand opening of The Getaway at Gee Bee Plaza, where a disc jockey would be on hand until closing.

Janet and Margie had met when Janet and her husband bought the house at 1184 Ella Street in Upper Monaca next door to the house that Margie shared with her husband, Joey. Their relationship epitomized that of most of the residents of these small communities tied together by the Ohio River and Interstate 376. Margie had known Janet's husband since childhood; they grew up across the street from each other. The homes they later bought in Upper Monaca were put up by the same builder, Colony Square Builders, owned by Gregory Scott Hopkins for whom Margie worked part-time cleaning houses.

"Obviously when they moved in, we knew Scotty (Walsh)," Margie would recall years later.

She remembered an idyllic small-town

world of friends and a slow and easy life.

"We had installed a swimming pool in our home, and back in those days, it's a lot different than today's world. In the summertime, your windows were open, your doors were open, garage door open. Our friends were always at our home. We had, you know, horseshoes set up, badminton in the backyard, the swimming pool. Our families were always there and all of our neighbors. We would always invite all of our neighbors. So it was just a fun place to be around. The kids had fun. You know, the kids would play baseball, and we were just always there. So, Scotty and Janet were there with us, you know, the four of us."

Janet, Margie said, developed a special relationship with Margie's son.

"She instantly just – she was wonderful to my son, absolutely wonderful with him, and it was almost like, you know, he used to call her Aunt Janet. She loved him very much, and he was very close to her."

Janet also would often drop in on Margie at work, bring her some lunch to the construction site; they would sit and talk things over, chat about life, children, work, and husbands. Then came Scott and Janet's separation in 1979, Janet's move to an apartment in town, in Lower Monaca, where Janet was living when the two friends met up that Friday evening of Labor Day weekend for a few drinks with Margie's sisters-in-law, Georgina Wilson (last name Beightley at that time) and Elaine Deluco.

Janet and Margie began the evening at the Top of the Mall before moving on to the Getaway, about a mile away at the Gee Bee Plaza, to meet the other two women.

"We were just trying to cheer her up," Margie recalled. "She was going through a divorce. So, I mean, it was just, you know, trying to have fun, a fun evening with her."

Georgina and Elaine arrived at the club between 10 and 11 p.m. to find Janet and Margie already there. Elaine recalled everybody having a drink and that Janet had gone to the dance floor with a man nobody knew. The bar was crowded and the music, if not the conversation, was loud.

"Kind of quiet," Georgina remembered of the mood among the four women. "I mean, I didn't really know Janet that much to, like, have a long conversation with her. We were just, like, talking back and forth. It was no partying or loudness or anything like that, just relaxing."

She also remembered Janet having gone to the dance floor with an unknown man; strangers tend to stick in memories in Monaca, because they are a rarity.

The women closed the bar, leaving about 2 or 2:30 in the morning. Georgina and Elaine went home; Janet and Margie walked to Perkins for a bite to eat. The stranger who had danced with Janet walked to the restaurant with them. The stranger, Margie recalled through a lens of distant memory, was looking for a ride home.

"It didn't make sense to me," she said, "because I didn't know him, and I didn't really follow it. I guess he had sat down at the booth, and it seemed like … he was talking more to Janet, and he thought he was going to be able to get a ride home, and she just kind of told him to move to another table. She – obviously, it sounds like she didn't want to be bothered with him."

The stranger moved to another table to sit

with other folks he apparently knew. Janet and Margie stayed at the restaurant until about four.

"By that time, after bars close, Perkins would get packed. So, it takes a while to get waited on, by the time you eat, you sit there, and get done."

Then, the two women went to the parking lot, each to their respective cars, and drove away, Margie to bed and then to attend a Labor Day weekend picnic for the Colony Square Builders' employees, Janet with no known plans for the next day other than to go to work.

It was the last that anybody, except her murderer, saw of Janet alive. It was the last anybody, except her murderer, would hear from her or of her – until the next day, when her father found her strangled to death in her bed and the police investigation of the first homicide anybody could recall in this community, about 45 minutes downstream from Pittsburgh, began. It was an investigation that would last for more than three decades.

2

Janet's closest friend, Barbara Cinderich, whom she'd known since seventh grade, provided law enforcement officials during their initial investigation the day of the murder with names and their connections to Janet. The first name she gave investigators was that of Gregory Scott Hopkins, the 33-year-old owner of the home construction company that had sold the Farinaccis their house and had built the Walsh home next door. He had met Janet through Margie Farinacci while she worked cleaning houses for his company.

"She talked to me about this guy, Scott Hopkins, that she's been seeing," Cinderich told officers. "She's separated from Scottie (Walsh), I think it was March. She's had this apartment of her own. Now, this Scott Hopkins built their house, up by the high school."

Hopkins, who went by his middle name of Scott, had been after Janet while Janet was still living with Scott Walsh, Cinderich said. "He kept asking her to go to bed and all that. And she wouldn't while she was married. Well since March, after she left Scottie (Walsh) and got into this apartment, she started seeing this Scott Hopkins."

Cinderich had been living with Janet for a little more than a week during this period, since moving back to Monaca from Pittsburgh, where she had lost her job as a nurse after getting caught stealing pain-killing drugs.

"Janet tells me everything," Cinderich told police. "I know everything that Janet does. So Janet's been seeing this Scott. But he only ... he's divorced ... and he's got a couple of girl friends. The only time she saw him was in the middle of the night. He'd just ... he'd call her ... he had Janet's apartment ... they never went anywhere, you know, never went out to dinner or anything like that. But he'd called her like at three or four in the morning and come down at that time. He had one thing on his mind. Yeah, and that was it."

Cinderich and Janet would sit on the porch, and lie in bed at night, and talk about their childhood, Janet's failing marriage, their friends and relationships – and Cinderich didn't like what she saw of how Hopkins was treating her friend.

"Just lately, in the last couple of weeks," she told police, "she said that she was getting tired of this, and that she didn't want to keep doing it. And we talked about it, and I said, you know, 'cause she's separated and this guy's divorced. I said, 'I don't care if he's got another girlfriend, he's still not married, you know. He can take you out to dinner and everything,' and the more she thought about it, she told him, he called a couple nights ago … I can't tell you what day it was … but it was in this past week, and it was late cause she was sleeping and he woke her up. When she talked to him she was really mad at him, and she just said 'I don't want to ever see you again. And just leave me alone,' and all that stuff. She was so quiet all the time and really reserved, and she said, she told me that she was surprised what she told him. She was, you know, like swearing at him and really mad."

But the dominant male personality in the drama of Janet's life at that time was, of course, the man to whom she was still married even though they were living apart. The police certainly didn't need for Cinderich to raise the possibility of Scott Walsh as the prime suspect, but she did, as the Hopkins conversation evolved.

"Janet never did anything to Scott Hopkins while she was married to Scottie," she told police. "But he ... he was suspicious because he got a couple phone calls like from this guy, and Janet did say that that's who it was, and she was scared that Scott (Walsh) would get mad, so ... he knew there was something going on."

So, police asked, "Hopkins was the only other man you know of in Janet's life at that time?"

"No, there's one more ... her boss, Ron Ciccozzi. He was only at the apartment once. And that was like ... two weeks ago, maybe last week."

"Did he stay overnight?"

"No," Cinderich responded, "He came down to fix her water heater or something."

Ciccozzi and Janet, Cinderich said, were "friendly ... long as they worked together."

The police wanted to know if Ciccozzi had come to Janet's apartment late at night or during the day.

"It was in the evening ... early evening, like six or seven. After she came home from work, she didn't have any hot water, and the pilot was out ... or something. And she just called him to come and light it."

"He wouldn't have a key to her place or anything?"

"No," replied Cinderich.

One of the state troopers investigating the case liked Ciccozzi for the crime, Gall would recall more than three decades later. Just a hunch. "He knew Ron Ciccozzi, their kids were going to school together, they had some interaction, and he just knew the guy, he thought it was him," Gall said of the trooper. Add in that Ciccozzi had run into Janet and Margie the evening before the murder at the Top of the Mall and had later been at the Getaway when Janet and Margie met their friends there. And then there was the set of keys belonging to Ciccozzi's Reliable Refrigeration, which Scott Walsh had found and dropped off at Janet's apartment.

But back then, Ciccozzi was just one of several names uttered in passing by relatives and friends of Janet trying to make sense of it all when he was called in by police to answer some questions.

Ciccozzi, who was married, admitted up front to having visited Janet in her apartment to fix her hot water heater.

"I was there about, I would say a good hour," he told police when they interviewed him. "I went down there, looked at the hot water tank, started it, adjusted the pilot on it and then went upstairs with her. She showed me around the apartment. We talked, oh, maybe 15 to 20 minutes."

He said the visit had occurred three weeks to a month before, and that nothing else had transpired between the two. She had worked for him for about 14 months, he said, and their relationship was "strictly on the boss-secretary level," though he said they were "close." That meant, he added, close in the office. "I never dated her. I never took her out. I saw her out," – meaning that he would see her in a club or out on a Friday night and he would, "buy her a drink or something. But I never took her out or anything, never left with her, you know, nothing like that."

He said he had never had a sexual relationship with her. Asked what he knew about her relationships with men, Ciccozzi said he didn't know anybody that she dated. Pressed about his relationship with her, which he again said was "close," and whether it had ever become sexual, he said Janet had asked him to take her out.

"To go out with her. I mean, you know, 'why don't you, why don't you go there, meet me at there, and have a drink or something.' I says, 'no I can't.' I says, 'I can't afford to do something like that.' And I never did. If I, if I saw her out and had a drink with her, it was just, it was no prearranged thing, I just happened to see her there."

And that was all that had happened when he saw her the eve of the murder, said Ciccozzi. He had offered to pay for Janet's and Margie's drinks at the Top of the Mall. But they passed on the offer, paying for their own drinks when they left to go to the Getaway, where Ciccozzi would again see them later that night – the night that Janet would visit the dance floor with the stranger in town, later identified for police by witnesses in the Getaway as Robert McGrail.

McGrail was the first man, on what eventually would become a five-man suspect list, that officers interviewed the afternoon of the murder.

In a rambling, somewhat incoherent interview, McGrail, who said he was working as a janitor at Woolworth's at the time, admitted after some questioning to having danced with Janet and walking to Perkins with her and Margie afterward. He had previously lived in Massachusetts, where he married and divorced, leaving two children behind, and in Texas.

He and a friend decided around 9:30 p.m. to go to the Getaway for a drink. His friend left about midnight, leaving McGrail without a ride home. He invited himself into the four-girl Walsh party.

"So I stayed until closing, and one of them kind of offered to give me a ride home. And so I think there was four girls, two of them went home and then the three of us went to Perkins and we ate, we ate a couple of sandwiches," he told officers. "They were married, you know, were just, you know, being friendly. … This one girl said that her husband might be … and so she had to … like eat with someone else … or I'd eat alone. So I said, okay, and I left the table."

He finished eating, paid his bill and walked home at about 3:30 a.m. to his rental house, where he lived by himself, below the campus of Penn State Beaver, he said. Late in the interrogation, McGrail remembered that one of the girls was named Janet.

Asked if he had become intoxicated, he recalled, "I was feeling good. I wasn't … intoxicated. I knew where I was, where I was going. I was just – I had a few drinks."

He thought the girls, Margie and Janet, had left Perkins before him, "or they may have possibly still been there … I just finished eating and I … I didn't want to look over at that booth to see if they had left or not … or if they was staying there … I don't know."

Near the end of the interrogation, McGrail remembered more details. At Perkins, he remembered being told by one of the girls that she didn't want her husband to see him.

"Yeah. … She … was one of the first ones I danced with. A fast dance … disco or something."

When he first joined the table of four girls and began to dance, police asked him, did he plan on taking one of them home with him?

"Well, I was just out dancing with them and that's all. I didn't have an intention of, you know …"

As the interview focus narrowed onto Janet, whom McGrail identified as the one with brown hair, the subject of dancing came up again. He was asked if they were fast dancing or disco dancing.

"We were just dancing regular and then regular dancing and then I asked if she wanted to disco … she said, yeah, and it didn't work out too well so … and she sat down."

"This particular lady," Cashdollar asked, "you say she couldn't disco very well? How do you know this is true?"

"I was taking lessons for about a year."

That night at Perkins was the last time he saw the woman he knew as Catherine Walsh, he said. After eating with another woman he knew in the restaurant, "I just walked out of Perkins, and there was, there's a hill, a very steep hill … the hill comes down this way, Brodhead this way, and then this way from the campus … and where it met, there was like a creek, and then there was like a wire, old wire fence. You could just step over that, and you'd be on my property, and I could go up to my home."

He went straight to bed, he said, "and slept heavily because, you know, I had been drinking that night, you know, um, and in the morning, must have been around ten, I'm just guessing, I can't remember exactly what time it was, the police were at the front door banging on the door, and they had the house with cruisers and all kinds of people there. Um, I didn't know what to make of it. You know, it startled me from sleeping. I just threw a pair of pants on. They asked me to come down; they wanted to question me about something. They did not say what it was until I got to the police station."

***

Seven days after the murder, a woman named Wanda Jesky turned in to police a checkbook she had found in a street gutter at the corner down the street from Janet Walsh's apartment. It was McGrail's checkbook, prompting police to bring him in for a second interrogation.

McGrail had no explanation for the checkbook; he stuck to his story.

So, after their interrogation of a suspect who admitted to having drunken designs on Janet Walsh, who was spurned by her, and who had no alibi for the morning of her murder, police turned their attention to the other two suspects identified by Barbara Cinderich: Gregory Scott Hopkins and her estranged husband, Scott Walsh.

Hopkins told police that he knew before coming in to headquarters the reason he was there "because a very good friend of hers was supposed to come to my house for a party, called me and talked about the murder. ... Farinacci called me and told me."

The first question after that was if Hopkins knew Janet and, if so, how well.

"Not well. I mean I don't, I mean, I've talked to her. I know her to see her. You know, talked to her relatives."

At that point, the interrogating officer cautioned Hopkins: "If you're going to talk about this at all, that you tell the whole story."

Then the officer asked Hopkins again how well he knew Janet.

"Well, I think I know what you're asking me. I have to answer in such a way that it doesn't mislead you either. I don't know her that well. I have been with her on occasions. I don't really, she's not a good friend. She's not a person I am dating or anything like that. But I have seen Janet a couple of times."

By that, he explained, "Mmm, been to her house. I guess that's what you want me to say. I talked to her on the phone or she stopped down, you know, and talked to me a couple times."

This was an apparent reference to the times that Janet had visited Margie Farinacci, sometimes bringing her lunch while Margie was at work cleaning houses for Hopkins' construction company.

The last time he had been to Janet's house, Hopkins said, had been three or four weeks prior.

Under what circumstances?

"I stopped to see her."

This stop, Hopkins said, was late, "like eleven. I'll try and remember 'cause I've only been down, like a couple of times. I'm trying to remember what a ... I can't remember what night."

Hopkins told the officers then that he had been to Janet's house two times, but that might be off by one time.

Asked if he'd ever had sexual relations with Janet, Hopkins responded with a "yes."

"Now," he continued, "I hope this is confidential ... because I could get into a lot of trouble over that."

Assured of the confidentiality of the conversation, Hopkins again stated that he had seen Janet a couple of times.

"You know, there was no emotional involvement. She just needed somebody to be around. She was going through a bad time. And I am involved with somebody and I am not interested in anybody else."

That person Hopkins was going with was a girlfriend he had been seeing for a long time while going through a divorce, which was not final at the time, from his first wife. He was now living in one of his model homes. At this point, the interrogation turned to Hopkins' whereabouts the previous night and that early morning.

"Alright," he responded. "I figured you were going to get to this, I have three witnesses that were just last night, were with me last night."

Detailing his activities of the previous evening, Hopkins told the officers he had been at his office and then, from 5:30 or 6 p.m. until 8 had gone water skiing. He then was at his office from 8 on, except for running out at 11 p.m. to pick up some supplies for a pig roast he was planning for his employees the next day.

Back to the subject of Janet, Hopkins was asked the latest he'd ever been at Janet's house and what kind of car he drove.

One-thirty or 2 o'clock, Hopkins responded, and he owned a Porsche, a Rabbit, three pick-up trucks and a Jeep Cherokee. Most of those, he said, were his corporation cars.

The questioning went back to the previous night. Hopkins was asked whom he was with. He said with Larry Musgrave, who worked with him at the construction company, Larry's wife, Georgina, and Hopkins' girlfriend, Dianne St. George.

The interrogating officer urged Hopkins to relax.

"She's upset 'cause I'm down here," Hopkins said. "She says, 'well, what're you going down there for?' I say, 'I don't know.' "

Hopkins then was asked who could vouch for him after 11 p.m. He told the officers that all three witnesses could, that they had spent the night with him.

"What happened, we had a pig roast today, so we prepared last night 'til like one to 1:30. And we got up around six, I don't know exactly what time it was. We got the fire going and you know, got it all heated up. Got the pig on around 7:30. And they all spent the night."

The police wondered if anybody else was

seeing Janet.

"As far as I know, she wasn't seeing anybody … What she told me was that she did not want to get involved with anybody, 'cause you know, she didn't, she wasn't totally emotionally together because, you know, her separation and everything. And she was not involved, wanting to get involved with anybody, from what she said to me. She didn't, you know, she didn't want to really date somebody or anything like that so far as I know, no. But, like I didn't talk to her every day. So I could be wrong but to my knowledge, I don't think so. Because she seemed to keep pretty much to herself. I know, like if she'd get lonely at night or something, she'd give me a call, you know, just to talk to me and a …"

Asked if he and Janet had ever argued, or if they had broken off, Hopkins said he hadn't talked to her for some time.

"It was only a couple of times. So I don't know if there was anything to break off."

"How many times did you?" Hopkins was asked.

"Two or three."

Hopkins told officers he had met Janet through Margie Farinacci. He said Farinacci worked for him but that she was not a girlfriend. However, he said, he and Musgrave had been out with Janet and Margie for drinks on Wednesday nights at the Holiday Inn, after builders' meetings.

The last time he'd spoken to Janet, he said, was when he had phoned her about a week before at 11 or 12 at night and woke her up.

"Okay, fine," Hopkins said. "I'll talk to you later," making no reference to the argument or ultimatum that Cinderich had referenced.

Hopkins told the officers that he did not have a key to Janet's apartment, though he'd known her for about two years; he had built the Upper Monaca house that Janet and her husband, Scott Walsh, had bought from a third party.

***

But Scott Walsh was the primary suspect of most of the officers.

"The thing with me was, this was my first

murder," Gall would recall later, "but the veteran guys there all said statistics show, experience shows, it's the husband or a boyfriend. And so he became the main suspect for Chief Conti, Bernie Cashdollar and the state policeman Frank Keenan."

Asked by police to recount his activities of the eve of his wife's murder, Scott Walsh told officers he had gone with a friend, who worked with him at the St. Joe Zinc Co., to Corsi's, arriving about 6 p.m., leaving about 7 p.m. to attend the Beaver Falls-Blackhawk football game. After the game, they stopped at Stubby's restaurant, and Walsh took his friend home at midnight. His friend became ill, and Walsh said he then took his friend to the Beaver Falls hospital emergency room, arriving home at about 2:05 in the morning. He had lived alone at the home on Ella Street since separating from his wife.

"And that's where I stayed until eleven o'clock this morning."

The next day – that morning – he said, he went out to run errands and then, while driving past his wife's house, he saw his father-in-law,

Peter Caltury, walking away from her house. He proceeded to Equibank and the post office. He owed his wife $75 support, he said, so he went back to her house.

"I went to the door and I rang the door bell. And I didn't get an answer so I put it in the mail slot. That's what she always told me to do."

He had found the set of Reliable Refrigeration keys in his backyard, which he put into the mail slot along with the check and a letter he had found outside.

Asked why he and Janet had separated, Walsh said, "she lost her job. We just had fights, and things like that, you know, just little things. We separated once and got back for a couple months and then we separated again, you know. The usual problems."

They had been married three years, he said, and had no children. He said he and Janet had sold their home on Ella Street in Upper Monaca.

Asked if his wife had been seeing anyone, he said he had been told that morning at the murder scene by Barbara Cinderich that Janet had been seeing someone.

"I didn't know that … she said she wasn't seeing anybody to me, but Barb said she was."

The man's name, Scott Walsh said, was Scott Hopkins.

"That's what Barb told me. He owns Colony Square Builders, where we bought our house from."

"How did the subject of Hopkins come up?"

"Well, we was talking to my father-in-law and everything, and just talking and everything, and I said, 'Barb, was she seeing somebody?' And she said, 'yes, she was.' And I said, 'I wonder who it is.' And she says, 'yeah.' And then, so she told me, on the walk, she told me."

Did he have any suspicions?

"Well, she hung out with Margie an awful lot and Margie, she worked out there. I think she does still work out there. And so I thought something was going on."

Walsh told police his wife had never accused him of running around.

"We were fighting over financial problems."

Police asked if Walsh knew what Hopkins looked like.

"He's short. I think he's about five-foot-nine-inches or so, five-foot-seven-inches. And I think he's going bald on top with black hair and he might have a hair piece, I don't know, I haven't seen him for a long time." Walsh said he thought Hopkins was in his 30s.

Scott Walsh and Janet had been high school sweethearts, Walsh told police.

"I was a sophomore in high school, when we started going together. She was a freshman."

Asked again about their relationship, Walsh said that when they separated, he didn't like the idea of Janet living by herself.

"You know, it wasn't that we were mad at each other, you know. We had a long talk together and everything."

Cinderich, in a subsequent interview, told police that the appraiser had been to the Walshes' Ella Street house that Friday before the murder, and Janet had told Cindrich that she had been to the house.

"And she was getting kind of sentimental about Scottie (Walsh). She said that she went up to the house and he had his three yearbooks that she never signed when they were in school, and she said that while she was at the house, she sat inside the house, went and sat in the backyard and just, like, looked for the last time, 'cause she had signed it away. And she left Scottie. She ... I don't know what she signed in the yearbooks, she just said it was mushy. That's what she said. And she left Scottie that note. She didn't tell me about that, but Scottie showed it to me then on Saturday. The note she had left him. And she said that, she just wanted to go out that night and have a good time.

"She said, 'I feel like dancing and just ... getting out of the house.' And she said, 'I've been thinking about Scottie a lot,' and she said, 'I know I love him but I'm just not sure that I want to go back with him yet.' "

Asked by police if she thought Janet Walsh would have let her husband in the morning of her murder, at 3 or 3:30 a.m., Cinderich said "no. I really don't. Not protecting Scottie or anything, but it's, like, when he asked her out on their anniversary, she felt bad 'cause she, you know, she was missing her anniversary and everything, but she still told him that she didn't want to go out to dinner. And he was kidding … he said something the other day, that now that they sold the house, he'd have to get an apartment. And she asked him one day, 'where you going to live?' And he was joking, and he said, 'I just thought I'd move back in with you.' You know, and said, 'no.' She said, 'you're not coming back.' "

Asked if she was aware that Scott Walsh had been seeing someone along about that same time, Cinderich said that Janet "thought she knew for a long time, and she was right."

Scott Walsh had been seeing a girl who was still in high school.

"And that was one of the things Janet always complained about Scottie, that he just never grew up, you know, like he wasn't real responsible. Like things that had to be done around the house and everything but she said that, you know, this girl's still, what I think she's a senior in high school and she's a cheerleader and everything and she said, 'I just, you know, can't believe it that Scottie has some interest in her.' But she did find out. And it was around their anniversary time, which was why she was so upset, when she found out for sure."

Cinderich told police that Janet used to complain that her husband "used to ride around the house after she got her apartment, all the time. And she worried about that like she worried about her mother and dad, you know, like when she was talking about Scott (Hopkins) or something, she said, 'well, if this car was here my mother would have to know whose car that was' and she said, 'Scottie's probably wondering the same thing.' And she said, 'really, he has no business riding around.' "

When she was living with Janet, Cinderich told police, "there was a couple nights when we were on the porch, I didn't know his car then, and by the time Janet said that was Scottie that went by, I didn't even know it. We were sitting on her porch and he came up, down the side of the school there and turned up Indiana, didn't come right past the house, he was up like the corner.

And I didn't know it was him until after he had already turned and was down the street."

Cementing his status as a prime suspect in the murder were the results of Scott Walsh's October 4, 1979 polygraph test, in which Beaver County Major Crime Task Force detectives Ray Salvati and Royal D. Hart concluded in their October 12 report: "It is our professional opinion that based on the reactions to the formulated questions, that the examinee was deceptive and has knowledge of and/or involvement in this criminal act." A second polygraph produced the same finding.

The polygraphs of Ciccozzi, Cinderich, Farinacci and McGrail concluded that there was no attempt at deception. Hopkins was not asked to take a polygraph test.

Meanwhile, as police investigators were following all of the leads, conducting interrogations and checking alibis, the local newspaper was reporting little progress in the investigation.

"Investigators probing the murder of 23-year-old Catherine Walsh of Monaca say they are still looking for a motive, but plan to stay on the case until it is solved," reported the Sunday,

October 7, 1979 Beaver County Times. "For the past five weeks, investigators have been questioning neighbors, friends, relatives and acquaintances of Mrs. Walsh, hoping to turn up a clue which would lead them to the killer.

"The one thing that has investigators puzzled is the killer's motive.

" 'It's particularly tough,' " one investigator noted, " 'because there is no obvious motive. We know it wasn't robbery; she wasn't sexually molested; and there was no heavy hate (on the part of the murderer) because she wasn't beaten.' "

One investigator, the newspaper reported, "doesn't believe that Mrs. Walsh returned home with the killer, or that the killer was already in the apartment that morning. 'There's nowhere in the apartment to hide and the locks were still on the doors,' when Mrs. Walsh's parents discovered her dead in her bedroom the next morning, a spokesman close to the investigation noted.

" 'We're not giving up, and we won't until we solve it,' " one investigator told the newspaper.

But, as Detective Gall would recall in 2014, the problem with this case was that there was more than one good suspect, but not enough evidence beyond circumstantial to tie any single one conclusively to the murder.

"Bizarre," he would say.

Cinderich, whom Gall would credit with being the most forthcoming witness of those who knew Janet Walsh, and who provided the most voluminous information to police, died in California from a drug overdose in 1997 and would never know who killed her best friend. And, as police continued to investigate, it appeared that neither would anybody else know the identity of the murderer – though Gall made a promise to Peter Caltury that he would, somehow, find the killer.

3

A year and a half after the murder, Janet Walsh's father and mother brought renewed attention to the case when they offered a $10,000 reward "for information leading to the arrest and conviction of their daughter's killer," according to The Beaver County Times.

An accompanying story, bannered across the top of the front page on February 8, 1981, reported that the murder trail was "cold, but far from forgotten."

"An inspirational message in Peter and Mary Jane Caltury's home in Monaca read, 'We must not sit down and wait for miracles; be up and going!' " began the story. "Were it only as simple as words."

" 'I guess that's what I should be doing,' conceded Mrs. Caltury. 'I try to keep myself busy, but it hurts; we will never be the same again. I can't be at peace until I know who did it and why. I still can't believe it.' "

The story then recounted the details of the murder and summarized the, "intensive investigation" of the previous seventeen months "in which police have scoured the quiet residential neighborhood for clues, administered polygraph tests and questioned nearly 300 people. Mrs. Walsh's death remains a mystery and her killer remains at large."

Bernard Cashdollar, coordinator of the Beaver County Major Crime Task Force, defined the investigation as the epitome of a cold case.

" 'We're still looking into possible leads and interviewing people,' " he told the newspaper. " 'But frankly, we're nowhere; we don't have anything to go on.' "

What police needed, Cashdollar said, was a motive, as there was no sign of a struggle or attempted robbery or sexual abuse.

" 'An ironing board at the foot of the bed would have fallen if there was (a struggle),' " he said. In some murder cases, he said, reports of a peeping Tom or of underwear thefts in the neighborhood bring some leads.

"The one lead which police were counting on, but which never materialized, was the report that a young man, clean-shaven and about 23 years of age, inquired from a neighbor directions to Mrs. Walsh's apartment about 8:30 the night she was killed.

"A composite sketch and a detailed description of the man was widely circulated, but his identity remains unknown. Cashdollar believes the young man may be significant to the case."

The officer was baffled, according to the newspaper.

"Cashdollar said one thing that puzzles him is that he questioned a woman living a short distance from the apartment house who, like the rest of her neighbors, heard nothing unusual that evening. The woman, he noted, was up reading until 4 or 5 a.m. because of insomnia. It was a balmy night, and the woman left her windows open to catch the breeze. She didn't hear a sound; neither did her watchdog."

Cashdollar offered a theory that Janet may have been taken by surprise, that someone strangled her accidentally "and then ran from the house."

Janet's mother, though, had a different theory.

" 'I have a feeling that she had been threatened and she expected to die,' " Mrs. Caltury told the newspaper, offering no details behind her suspicion.

"In her deepest moments of depression, Mrs. Caltury sometimes turns to an old friend, Mrs. Jean Batto of New Sewickly Township, for comfort. Mrs. Batto and Mrs. Caltury were childhood friends in Monaca Heights," the story continued. "Like her friend, Mrs. Batto and her husband are grieving. It was in November of 1977 that someone broke into the mobile home of William and Nancy Adams, the Battos' daughter and son-in-law in Fallston, and killed William with a shotgun blast and abducted Nancy. The Battos are still searching for their daughter."

Like the police, Mrs. Caltury was mystified because of the lack of apparent motive.

" 'She was a good girl; she was sickly and led a sheltered life,' " she told the newspaper.

" 'She had high principles; she was more of a homemaker than a night person. She only went out that night to get some entertainment. She would have never hurt anyone; if anyone deserved to live, it was her. I would rather it had been me than her.' "

She said the discovery of her daughter's body would haunt her for the rest of her days.

" 'That moment will never leave my mind,' said Mrs. Caltury. 'My husband and I entered Janet's apartment through the back door. Janet was in her bed, the covers were pulled up around her shoulders to her neck; we thought she was sleeping. I said to my husband, "aren't you going to wake her up, dad?" He tried but she didn't wake up. We couldn't see the scarf, at first; he reached down and felt the lump and then saw that her hands were tied with the bathroom cord.

" 'My husband pulled me away, but I didn't believe him. I went back and shook her – "wake up, wake up" – but she didn't wake up. I hope no parent ever has to go through what we have.' "

***

Detective Andrew Gall had stayed in touch with the Calturys, and they with him, over those years and later on.

"It was my first real murder," Gall would recall in his office on the second floor of the Beaver County courthouse. "I get this murder, and I meet the Calturys, Mr. and Mrs. He was always a very friendly guy, not overly friendly, he was more welcoming, she was like almost in shock, and she loses her twenty-three-year-old daughter."

A picture of Gall leaning over an elderly, smiling Peter Caltury is on the wall just to the right of Gall's computer. Other pictures and plaques hang on the walls surrounding Gall in his small office across the hall from District Attorney Anthony Berosh: a photo of a totaled car resting in front of a semi truck – his first fatality, one of two fatalities and two suicides that would be his most major cases before the Walsh murder.

A framed movie poster hangs to the left of his computer wall. It depicts an old Humphrey Bogart flick, "You Can't Get Away With Murder." He and his wife bought it late in the Walsh murder investigation, found it in a second-hand store "for a buck," Gall said. "My wife said, 'this is an omen.'"

A Morgan Crain painting of cowboys riding horses in a stream hangs on the wall opposite his desk: "I was born 100 years too late," says the 6-foot-1, wiry, 185-pound bespeckled Gall. "I should have been a cowboy."

Gall caught the murder case as a 25-year-old, working it first with state Trooper Rich Matas, who got transferred and handed the case to Trooper Frank Keenan. At the request of the police chief, Gall kept the case after he left the Monaca Police Department to take a private security job with a local steel firm for a lot higher salary while still doing part-time duty with local police departments. But bored by gate security work, he returned to law enforcement full-time, joining the force of his home town police department in Baden. Monaca kept him on as an active part-time police officer "so that I could continue to work this case … and I would continue to work with the state police.

"Keenan was a guy, who was called 'Smooth,' because he's just a very compassionate state trooper," Gall recalled. Mrs. Caltury, he said, would call Keenan, and "Mr. Caltury would call me. Even after I left Monaca, Mr. Caltury had my home number, plus I would call him, at least for a while, during the real slow periods when nothing was happening, it would be twice a year, just to call, touch base, he would call me, he would call the Monaca station and I would get a call, because I would always stay in touch with the Monaca guys, even when I left there.

"He was always open and willing to answer questions," Gall said of Caltury. "He never made it an adversarial relationship, he was just seeking information, to make sure somebody still cared and paid attention, so we would talk regularly, particularly after I started here (as a detective reporting to the Beaver County district attorney) in '88, he would call here, and he had my inside number, and when cell phones came in, I gave him my cell number, and he would just call me whenever."

The two would talk about family and friends.

"He'd tell me about his two boys, how they were getting along," Gall said, adding that he would assure Caltury that he and the other investigators were still looking at all the suspects.

"I'd stop up to his house over the years because he'd never left that part of Monaca, up on the hill, and just chat with him, even as the years went on."

***

But then an unexpected turn in the Walsh murder investigation came in 1983, when a new suspect entered the case, a man we shall call Carlo (this suspect's name has been changed – the only character in this book whose name is not real). For Gall, Carlo quickly became a primary suspect who had been in the area for a relatively short while, with only a brief encounter with the victim – if there was any encounter at all.

The investigation into Carlo began with a suspicious incident. Evidence of Carlo's whereabouts on the eve and morning of the murder and his curious behavior after that time increased the suspicion.

"If you had asked me in 2008 to list who I thought would have done this," Gall would later recall, Carlo "for me was at the top."

In January of 1983, a woman went to the Monaca police to tell them she was waitressing at Johnny's Family Restaurant in downtown Monaca in late November when Carlo came in.

"He was coming in every night that I worked," the 31-year-old woman, who lived on the same street as Janet Walsh's apartment but a block away, told police in a voluntary statement. "He asked me to go to a concert with him. I told him I was sorry, but I was married. He became very angry with me. He said if I was married I should have rings on, which I did not. He was extremely upset. He said, 'I would not ask a married woman out. You must think I think you are a harlot.' I got up from the table and went to the counter, he followed me. He became very calm.

Suddenly he said, 'I was out with the girl who was strangled in Monaca.' I said 'who?' He said 'Janet Walsh. You remind me of her. You have the same hair and eyes like her.' My hair is long, but on that night I had it up.

"I asked him if he dated her, he said he took her out two days before her murder. He started to describe the murder. He said she was choked real tight ... and he then looked down at the floor like he was in a trance and shook his head and repeated two times 'not a hair out of place, it was like I wasn't even there.' We were interrupted and the subject changed.

"The cook came out of the kitchen and asked what we were talking about. I said Janet Walsh's murder. She said they would never catch the killer and (Carlo) said they probably never will. (Carlo) also mentioned in the conversation that she lived in the house across from the school."

Police learned that Carlo had been dropped at his second-floor apartment near Janet's street, after the bars had closed the morning of the murder. Chief Conti and Gall had interviewed a woman who had been with three other women at the Getaway late the Friday night and early the Saturday morning of the Walsh murder.

"She remembers conversing with Janet Walsh and also remembers giving (Carlo) a ride home from the Getaway to the Dairy Queen parking lot" in downtown Monaca, states the transcript of that January 20, 1982 interview. "She had left the Getaway at approximately 2:20."

Walsh's friend Margie Farinacci in an interview later that same day told officers that though Walsh knew Carlo and had introduced him to her once at the office, "she says that Walsh made a statement of some kind about his mental condition at the time and she doubts that she would have dated him," according to the transcript of that interview.

That mental condition may have been related to a 1978 accident, according to police reports, that led to treatment by a Pittsburgh doctor, who told police that he remembered Carlo's case, "very well because it was so unusual and it stemmed from his accident in July of 1978. (Carlo) had a couple of major operations on his head and brain area and also treatment involving the blood supply to the brain," the doctor, who treated Carlo from October 9 of 1978 to October of 1979, told police. "He has no record of any abnormalities or unusual behavior on his psychological work-up. He remembers no odd behavior and says that although black-outs could occur due to any head injury he doubts (Carlo) suffers from them."

The doctor told police that he wrote a paper on this particular patient that was published in a national journal.

Monaca police continued their investigation into Carlo when they contacted a 25-year-old female acquaintance in Aliquippa, who told police during a January 17, 1983 interview that Carlo had met her when he worked as a bartender at the establishment where she had come to pick up lunch for some girlfriends at work. Carlo reportedly then visited her at her work place.

"The subject would sneak around the rear of the boro building and come upstairs to talk to her and keep her from her work," according to the report. "He knew of her marital problems and says that he is waiting for her to leave her husband. He seems very persistent and strange to her and always looks around when talking to her as if he doesn't want anyone else to hear. About 2 weeks ago Boro Manager Tom Stoner told him to stay away unless he had business but he continued to call her during lunch time and this morning he stopped up at app. 8:30 AM to say hi!"

Then, during a police interview nine days later, a woman who also had been with the group of women at the Getaway on the evening preceding the murder told Gall that she remembered seeing Carlo at the disco that night, and "it is entirely possible that they gave him a ride."

On February 15 of 1983, Gall and a fellow officer interviewed a hostess at the Perkins restaurant in Center Township who told them she had met Carlo there some years prior.

"About 3 years ago," according to the transcript of that interview, "he followed her home from Perkins but was not able to discover where she lived. He had a habit of putting money (tips) into her apron pockets and approximately one year ago he grabbed her leg when doing this and she asked the manager … to make him leave."

The manager told Carlo, a regular customer, not to return until he could behave.

"He is now permitted in the restaurant but the employees all consider him 'strange.' "

During a February 18, 1983 interview with Monaca police, Carlo said he had moved to California in July of 1980 and returned on December 20, 1981. According to the transcript of that interrogation, "(Carlo) states he met Walsh approximately one week before the homicide. He went to Reliable Refrigeration to apply for a job ... Walsh gave him an application and he stayed about a half hour filling it out. He remembers talking about her car and remembers it was a lime green Monte Carlo with a white top. Carlo states he had seen her car on the 900 block of Indiana Ave. and felt she lived near there. He asked a few people about her and says he would have liked to date her. (Carlo) went back to Reliable a second time that week to check on his application. He also states he saw her drive past him a few times. (Carlo) does not remember seeing her at the Getaway the night of the homicide. He vaguely remembers being out there but doesn't remember riding home with (the woman who drove him home)."

Carlo seemed to enjoy women associated with eating establishments. In August of 1983, Gall and Conti interviewed a former girlfriend of Carlo's, a waitress, and learned of violent behavior tied to lovemaking and alcohol.

"She stated she met (Carlo) while working at Johnny's Restaurant in about November of 1982 and became friendly with him. They dated several times and she felt he could not perform sexually without drinking. He also always attempted to get her intoxicated before sex. He tried to get very possessive of her during the relationship and he became very argumentative when drinking.

"In late April of 1983, he struck her across the face with an open hand during an argument and she would not date him after although he tried to make amends. He fancies himself as a great lover and slept with her sister … to try to 'get back' at (her).

"She fears (Carlo) somewhat and does not like to be with him. On one recent occasion at the Band Room he grabbed her and kissed her very roughly and she attempted to push him away. She states he had a 'strange look in his eyes.' "

In March of the next year, a woman who had been dating Carlo contacted police to report her fear that he might kill himself.

"I was just talking to my boyfriend and he is very depressed and he said he was going to jump off the bridge," she told police, identifying Carlo by name and by where he worked as a bartender.

A Monaca police officer found Carlo about ten minutes later.

"While on patrol, I observed (Carlo) traveling west bound on Penna Ave.," the officer reported. "I followed (Carlo) to a parking stall on 10th Street. I asked (Carlo) if there was anything bothering him tonight. He informed me that everything was fine. I informed (Carlo) that our door is open if he needed to talk to somebody, he again informed this officer that everything was alright and he had no problems."

In a subsequent interview, the same girlfriend told police that she had met Carlo the previous August "and has dated him several times since. She states she thinks a lot of (Carlo) and feels his problems stem from problems with his family life. (She) feels that (Carlo) is still very depressed. She is aware that his father was 'very upset' about the suicide threat but taunts (Carlo) about it instead of offering to help. This interview ended at this time, as (Carlo) arrived at her apartment."

Later that year, Monaca police contacted the Whittier, California police department by letter to check on Carlo's record while he had been living there.

"Our homicide involves a young white female who was separated from her husband and lived alone," said the letter. "She was at a local nightclub and left the club alone. (Carlo) was also at the nightclub that evening and later investigation revealed prior contact with the victim and an alleged attraction for her.

"A check locally of (Carlo's) background and prior contacts show him to have a strange and somewhat violent relationship with females," the letter continued. "We request that you check your records for any unsolved violent crimes which may have occurred during the above time period (July 1980 until December 21st of 1981) that may have involved (Carlo)."

In November of 1984, Monaca Patrolman Gall wrote up a report relating his conversation with a Whittier police officer who relayed a chilling tale of a murder in his jurisdiction.

"Off. Gall talked to Det. Mel Otterman of the Whittier Police Department," Gall wrote in his report. "He reports that his homicide victim worked as a secretary-receptionist at the Presbyterian Hospital and this position placed her in contact with the public. She had a 'super- friendly' personality and would pick up men if she liked their looks. She was not a prostitute but was somewhat 'loose.'

"The victim had spent the evening with a girlfriend and visited a pizza shop. She was home alone. There is a possibility the killer entered the apartment by a window but he was probably let in by the victim. The victim was strangled with bare hands and raped. The pillows on the bed were left in a T shape.

"Otterman has some usable prints found at the scene. A copy of the initial report and all information on (Carlo) were sent to Otterman along with selected crime scene photos. Otterman checked with (Carlo's) landlord in Whittier who remembers him as shy and backwards. He remembers a girl from the east staying with (Carlo) for about 2 weeks but she left 'disgusted'."

After that, Carlo moved to Maryland in late 1985 or early 1986, according to police.

It was no wonder, then, that Gall saw him as a prime suspect in the Walsh murder, especially considering his residential proximity to her apartment and his getting dropped off near there, after an evening of clubbing, the morning of the murder.

"So he's getting dropped off at that intersection right about the time that Janet is getting home, she easily could have passed him up," Gall recalled. "We know she knew him and he knew her because he's gone in there (Reliable Refrigeration) a couple of times, but we didn't know that at the time of the initial investigation. So later when we realized she knows him, we started putting together that he could have waved her down, recognized her car, she pulls over and ends up inviting him. So he looked really good."

Carlo continued to look good even after he moved away. He had agreed to take a polygraph test, until a prominent local defense attorney informed police that Carlo would not be taking a polygraph and that officers were not to speak to Carlo again. He did not leave the police department's radar, however, until much later.

***

Meanwhile, the press from time to time would update the investigation.

The Beaver County Times in a story published August 31, 1984, reminded its readers that "The Walsh case hasn't been forgotten."

"At 28, Catherine Janet Walsh's life would hold promise," began the story. "But that was lost on a September morning five years ago when the 23-year-old Monaca resident was found strangled in her four-bedroom apartment on Indiana Avenue. No one has been arrested for her murder.

"Today, promises are still being kept for Catherine. Monaca Police Chief Lawrence Conti has vowed to solve the crime that baffles law enforcement authorities with unanswered 'whys.' "

Conti assured the reporter that the investigation "is never going to stop. 'I'll never quit working on it until I get to the bottom of it.' "

The chief was hesitant to discuss the case, according to the report, but Conti said "some progress has been made. 'I can't really say, but we've pursued a number of things. We've conducted interviews over the last year and a half. We're really at a standstill.' "

Walsh's parents lived daily with the "sense of their daughter's unfulfilled promise" cited in the story's lead paragraph, the newspaper reported.

" 'It gets worse after the years because you miss her so much.' Mrs. Caltury said. 'She was so young ... she didn't get to enjoy life. It was taken away from her.'

"Five years have elapsed, yet not a day passes, Mrs. Caltury says, when she doesn't think about her daughter.

" 'I'm still questioning why? I want to know who and why because there was no reason for this,' she said. 'She would not have hurt anyone. She was a good person.' "

Mrs. Caltury called the Monaca police frequently the first few months after the homicide, the newspaper reported. "Now, she calls every six months.

" 'I'm optimistic,' she said. 'I feel relieved after talking to the police. I don't bug them. I don't call them when I hear things through the grapevine. We are the last people to hear things. I wonder if people remember; but if there was any information, we would be the last people to hear.' "

Mrs. Caltury told the newspaper that she had disposed of most of Janet's belongings, "and tends to the needs of her husband and two sons."

She spends most of her time at home occasionally painting and making crafts.

" 'You have to make your own life,' " she told the newspaper. " 'I have to get up and get going and not dwell upon it,' she said. 'I have lots of time to think.' "

***

Time, though, had not altered the nightmare of the death of a loved one, said the headline of an August 4, 1991 Beaver County Times story that took a look at numerous unsolved murder cases in the area.

"Grief is not always diminished by time," began the story. "For some, the death of a loved one hurts as much 12 years afterward as it does 12 days later. When violence and mystery cloak that grief, it is magnified.

"Almost 12 years after someone viciously murdered her daughter, Mary Jane Caltury is quick to cry. Hers are not the sobs of new loss.

"She cries agonizing tears over the unanswered questions: Why? Who?

" 'We miss her so much,' she says of Catherine Janet Walsh. 'Not a day goes by that something doesn't remind me of her. I walk over to her sewing machine and sometimes, it's just too much. I can't finish what I'm working on.' "

Walsh's murder, reported the newspaper, was one of nearly two dozen unsolved homicides in the region "that continue to baffle local and state police. They are not cases that are pushed to the back of a file drawer. Instead, they remain thorns in the sides of investigating officers, some who remember details of the crimes without having to refer to notes."

Gall was one of those officers, telling the newspaper that he kept a 2-inch thick file folder in the top drawer of his desk.

"But he doesn't need to open it to tell you about the case.

"As late as last year, he chased a tip he thought might be a new lead. It turned out to be another dead end.

" 'Before I retire,' Gall says, 'I'd like to make an arrest on this case.' His voice comes close to sounding like a threat."

The police chief of nearby Hopewell Township told the newspaper that he understood Gall's frustration; two unsolved murders were on his police logs – one of them that occurred when he, too, was just a patrolman.

" 'What bothers me most is that someone just like you and me is walking around with this on their conscience,' " Fred David told the reporter. " 'How do they sleep?' "

Justice Delayed

One of those cases was the murder of 23-year-old Annette Rose Tokarz, whose body was found in a creek at Lakewood Park on March 4, 1974.

" 'Someone held her face down in about eight inches of water with such force that she inhaled sand and gravel into her lungs,' David says. 'After she was dead, her killer turned her over.' "

The dead woman was a Bridgewater resident. Similar to the Walsh case, there were no signs of sexual assault.

" 'It did appear that she had struggled with someone,' David says. 'She looked like she had been beat up and there was a gash on her breast. The area sometimes served as a make-out spot and we thought she might have gone there with someone and then tried to get away. We never found her purse.' "

There were other similarities to the Walsh case. Police had several suspects in the case, among them "several men friends." A polygraph test of one of them "indicated he had 'definite guilty knowledge of the crime.' But police got little more out of him." And, as in the Walsh case after Carlo became a suspect in the 1980s, police pressure brought a phone call from the man's attorney.

" 'Either we had to charge him or we would face a harassment complaint,' David says. 'We didn't have the evidence to file any charges.' "

The other unsolved case cited by David was the murder of a 39-year-old Hopewell High School English teacher found dead behind the wheel of his car on August 28, 1981. He had been shot with a 12-gauge shotgun.

" 'We believe it was a contract killing,' " David told the reporter. " 'Our theory is that he had himself killed. We found several people he solicited for the job. He told them he had terminal cancer. But we could never substantiate that … Someone's walking around out there who took money to kill that man.' "

The Walsh killing and these other two slayings were three of the 16 murders or suspicious deaths spotlighted by the newspaper's story that day, ranging in dates from the 1974 murder of Tokarz to the 1990 fatal shooting of 39-year-old

Carolyn Bradley of Hanover Township, killed while working as a clerk at an Independence Township convenience store.

An accompanying story, headlined "Police never give up on a case," explained how police approach these sorts of crimes.

State police review so-called cold case unsolved murders every six months, the newspaper reported, a process that mirrored the meticulous pursuit of state and local police investigating the Walsh case.

"They pull out folders stuffed with pages of notes, typed reports, transcribed interviews and names of suspects. And they decide if it's time to go back out and ask some more questions."

" 'We wait,' " Cpl. John Gallaher, Brighton Township crime unit supervisor, told the newspaper. " 'We are persistent. And we are methodical. We have good interviewers who keep going back and talking to people.

" 'Maybe an anniversary of the murder is coming up. Or the victim's birthday. There are dates that might have a psychological effect on someone, whether it's just a witness or relative who might be moved to remember something new, or a suspect whose conscience might be bothering him.' "

Officers play a "waiting game," Gallaher said. " 'The facts are there. The circumstances just have to be right for us to find them. If nothing else, they get the idea we are not going away.' "

That waiting game had already consumed four years by the time Gall had identified Carlo as a fifth viable suspect in 1983, and it would continue for another three decades as he relentlessly pursued it, Javert-like – except that the stolen bread of "Les Miserables" was not the crime of interest here; rather, it was the stolen life of a 23-year-old woman, with no discernible motive.

It was a waiting game that would see Janet Walsh's mother die in 2004 never knowing the identity of her daughter's killer – a passing that Gall believes was at least partly abetted by the frustration of not knowing why her daughter had died, let alone who had done it.

But then, along came a scientific and technological forensics breakthrough in the 1980s that would shine new light into the dark, sex- and alcohol-tinged recesses of this murder case and remove four of the five suspects – including Carlo – from Gall's list of possible killers.

4

The murders of Janet Walsh and of an Augusta, Maine woman named Blanche M. Kimball share a few common elements. Both occurred in the 1970s and thus constituted a couple of the nation's longest so-called cold cases on record. Both women were found slain in their homes with their clothing pulled up on their bodies. Police were called to both homes after someone concerned about their well-being began checking on them. Police found no signs of forced entry into the women's homes, and the doors of both homes were locked. Both were childless. And a new development in forensic science, DNA analysis, would play a key role in finding their killers.

The decomposing body of Kimball, a 70-year-old retired dental technician and practical nurse with no known close relatives, was discovered by police who responded on June 12, 1976 to a complaint from a neighbor who had not seen Kimball in several days, according to the October 17, 2012 Kennebec Journal.

"Kimball's clothing was pulled up and her body was decomposing," the newspaper reported. "The house was in upheaval, scattered with broken glass and debris." It was a brutal murder. The chief medical examiner reported that Kimball had been stabbed 23 times in the chest, twice in the abdomen, and that she had suffered "16 cuts and lacerations to the head, and three cuts and abrasions to the hands."

Police had a suspect in the case, a homeless man who had once rented a room from Kimball. Sixty-three-year-old Gary Sanford Raub had been a suspect early on, the newspaper reported. Raub had left Augusta after the slaying, but he had been caught during an attempted house break-in near Kimball's residence before he left.

"Police interest in Raub rekindled after he was accused in an October 2011 stabbing in Seattle that injured another homeless man," the newspaper reported. The police tested blood from the victim's kitchen for DNA and determined it was from a male, and then they analyzed DNA found on a knife used in the Seattle stabbing. "The analysis showed partial profiles were linked to Raub and to the blood found in Kimball's home," according to the newspaper, and a DNA analysis told an investigating officer that " 'the estimated probability of selecting an unrelated individual at random from the FBI Caucasian population data base is 1 in 339 million.' "

A bit of police ingenuity was used to obtain a DNA sample from Raub.

"An undercover officer with Seattle police then got a DNA profile from Raub in July by asking him to participate in a 'chewing gum survey,' " the Journal reported. "Tests showed DNA from the gum was consistent with samples found in Kimball's kitchen and on the knife handle from the Seattle stabbing."

As of this writing, Raub had been extradited to Maine. A statement by Jared Mills, then deputy chief of the Augusta Police Department, offered the newspaper a sentiment that, like many of the circumstances of many such cases, is common and timeless:

"'The public needs to know these cases never go away. This is a 36-year-old case that we didn't give up on. We'll never give up.'"

The evolving science of DNA makes giving up less of an option. DNA researchers credit Cambridge University research fellow James Watson and graduate student Francis Crick for development of DNA – which had first been detected in 1868 – as a forensics tool when the two scientists identified the double helix in their lab in 1953. Their research focused on the two types of acid in the nucleus of living cells: ribonucleic acid (RNA) and deoxyribonucleic acid (DNA). As explained by Katherine Ramsland in her exhaustive 2004 DNA primer, "The Science of Cold Case Files," 23 pairs of chromosomes in a cell's nucleus comprise DNA, "which acts as a blueprint to dictate our physical functions and characteristics.

"The 'instructions' are issued in a genetic code transferred from our parents, and these are unique to each person." Four nucleotide bases in the DNA "form the rungs of what looks like a ladder – the double helix," Ramsland, a professor of forensic psychology at DeSales University, wrote. "When strung together in these paired chromosomal stands," she continued, the four bases align so as to create the protein and enzyme composition of cells.

"A segment of DNA that arranges the amino acids into protein is called a gene, and when scientists refer to our entire collection of genes, they use the term genome. The genome tells the body what to do."

Most of these genetic "instructions" are common to all humans, Ramsland wrote, but a tiny percentage of certain gene sections – about 0.01 percent – carry the coding that makes each individual unique.

"These variations in base sequence are called polymorphisms, and the polymorphic DNA regions continually repeat," she wrote. "The base pairs in these regions are called variable number of tandem repeats, or VNTRs, and they provide the possibility for genetic identification.

"By looking at the parts of the DNA that make a person unique, experts can determine whether a particular strand of DNA found in a biological specimen is indistinguishable to an overwhelming statistical probability from the DNA of a particular person. Some people call that making a match, but since it's stated as a statistical probability, the 'match' is not entirely exact."

In 1986, British geneticist Alec Jeffreys discovered what he dubbed "DNA fingerprinting" when he made the genetic markers radioactive and X-rayed them. "Once the X-rays were developed, he saw the patterns of gray and black bands, which looked like grocery store bar codes, that would soon be recognized as the genetic signature," Ramsland wrote. Jeffreys' mappings of individual profiles were consistent "across different types of body cells, from blood to saliva to skin."

Jeffreys' breakthrough led to the first-ever murder investigation that featured the two most publicized and prominent outcomes of DNA analysis in criminal investigations – exoneration of persons wrongly accused of crimes, and the conviction of suspects in major, violent criminal cases, often after these cases had gone cold because of the lack of solid evidence, which is the focus of this book.

Police in Leicestershire, England contacted Jeffreys seeking his assistance in their investigation of two unsolved murders: the 1983 rape and murder of a 15-year-old girl in the village of Enderby and a murder three years later of a teenage girl in the village of Narborough.

According to the account of these investigations in Liz Porter's 2011 book, "Cold Case Files," police had taken into custody a 17-year-old kitchen porter who worked in a local mental facility.

"He had been spotted around the time of the 1986 murder in an area close to the lane where the body was later found; he knew details about the body that had not been released to the public; and he had a history of mental illness," Porter wrote. "Already emotionally disturbed, the intimidated teenager cracked under police questioning and confessed to the second murder. But he denied any involvement in the first."

Police asked Jeffreys to analyze the suspect's blood and semen samples obtained from the victims.

"The DNA profiles of the two victims' samples matched each other, but they didn't match the suspect's profile – a result that shocked both the detectives and the scientist," Porter wrote. "Thinking his technology might have failed, Jeffreys arranged for the Home Office's Forensic Science Service to do additional testing to check the results. They were correct. Like many emotionally vulnerable suspects before and since, the 17-year- old had been unable to deal with the pressure of being under suspicion and had made a false confession. Much to the relief of his parents, he was released."

In her analysis of this case, Ramsland concluded that the investigators "decided that the man had probably come upon the body, enabling him to use what he had seen to give them the impression that he knew more than he should have if he were innocent. Based on what he had said about it, they had simply worked him into a confession."

But police still had two unsolved crimes.

Impressed with this newfangled DNA

technology – Jeffreys' analysis found that the murders had been done by the same person – they enlisted Jeffreys to help them carry out what Porter called "the world's first DNA manhunt" in which all of the men of nearby villages with type A blood were asked to volunteer for a DNA test. Some 5,000 of them did so, "but the object," wrote Ramsland, "was to find any man who did not willingly submit, because that could indicate he had something to hide.

"That man was soon revealed," wrote Ramsland. "Colin Pitchfork, who had once been arrested for indecent exposure, had persuaded a friend to go to the test site in his place. Pitchfork provided his friend with a false passport, but the friend had a big mouth. When he bragged about what he had done, a woman who overheard him told police. That placed the spotlight dead on Pitchfork. After questioning, he confessed, and his genetic profile proved to be statistically indistinguishable from that of semen samples from both crimes. In 1987 he became the first person to be convicted of murder based on genetic fingerprinting."

The conviction gained worldwide attention for a revolutionary crime-solving technique.

"A person's unique genetic profile could be revealed from a small sample of his or her cells and compared against biological evidence from a crime scene," Ramsland wrote. "If this was a sure-fire technique, as it certainly appeared to be, that meant a complete transformation in crime scene analysis. And not just in the future. Those cases that had stalled but that still had preserved biological evidence could also be revisited for possible resolution. All that was required was to have the proper lab techniques and a suspect against whom to compare the evidence."

Indeed, Porter wrote, the Pitchfork case, buttressed by reports of the phenomenal statistical strength of DNA evidence, spawned a "slow trickle of DNA-based court cases."

In November of 1987, a man accused of rape in the United Kingdom "pleaded guilty after a scientist's report suggested that the chance of another person having the same DNA profile as the crime scene one would be expected to be 1 in 4 million."

The next year, Tommie Lee Andrews became the first U.S. citizen convicted using DNA evidence.

In the early morning hours of March 1, 1987, a woman telephoned Orlando, Florida police to report a peeping Tom. Responding officers saw a man matching the description driving in the woman's neighborhood. The driver sped away after the officers tried to pull him over, and a car chase ensued, ending when the suspected prowler rammed his car into a light pole. The capture of the suspect, reported the Orlando Sentinel on August 3, 2012, "would change the course of history."

The arrest of Andrews that day culminated a nearly four-month stakeout in 1987 and 1988 aimed at apprehending a man suspected to be a serial rapist tied to at least 16 cases.

"The attacks were similar," according to the newspaper. "The suspect wore a mask and would get into his victim's home through an unlocked window or door between midnight and 7 a.m. He would arm himself once he got into the home and told several of the victims that he had been watching them."

The newspaper reported that prosecuting attorney Jeff Ashton approached former Assistant State Attorney Tim Berry, assigned to prosecute Andrews, "about an emerging science known as DNA testing that he'd read about in a magazine article about paternity testing.

"Berry decided to give the new science a shot," reported the newspaper. "The state hired a private lab to test evidence in Andrews' cases, and the DNA matched."

The result was a conviction, as reported in a brief story in The New York Times dated February 6, 1988.

"Mr. Andrews, 24 years old, was convicted of breaking into the home of a 27-year-old Orlando woman, raping and stabbing her on May 9, 1986," according to the report. "The woman identified Mr. Andrews during the trial as her attacker." Andrews was sentenced to 100 years, later reduced to 51 years.

Case after case, DNA-based convictions accumulated. In February of 1989, a London man was convicted of murder based on a DNA analysis of mucus on a handkerchief he had dropped on a footpath after he strangled a 22-year-old woman. That same year, Australia had its first case involving DNA evidence; Desmond Applebee, "facing three counts of sexual assault, changed his story after his DNA, extracted from a blood sample, matched a profile taken from stains on the victim's clothing," wrote Porter. "He went from denying he was there to claiming that the sex had been consensual. But he was convicted."

Also in 1989, a serial rapist pleaded guilty to 18 counts of rape and was sentenced to 18 years after Victorian police in 1988 "obtained DNA evidence tying convicted thief George Kaufman to a series of rapes in Melbourne's southeastern suburbs from 1982 to 1986," according to Porter.

But one problem, Porter wrote, was that the testing techniques used to convict this rapist "could produce results only in cases where the evidence included relatively large amounts of biological material – a blood stain the size of a 20-cent piece or a semen stain the size of a 5-cent piece. And the process was slow and laborious."

Progress in DNA testing methods would

help overcome such problems. In 1986, U.S. researcher Kary Mullis developed polymerase chain reaction (PCR), or "molecular photocopying," which came into broad use in 1991 in the United Kingdom and in the United States and was adopted by the FBI in 1992.

"By 1994," Porter wrote, "with further developments in PCR, scientists began using areas of the DNA molecule known as short tandem repeats (STRs) or 'micro-satellites.' Shorter sections of DNA than the previously used minisatellites, several of them could be copied at the same time and the system could work with bloodstains a mere two millimeters square."

Also in 1994, forensic scientists in the United Kingdom began using SGM, "a commercial kit which used PCR to analyse six different sites – or loci – on the DNA, along with a marker which told the gender of the sample's owner at the same time. Each 'locus' has two 'alleles,' one from each of the DNA owner's parents. Test results were expressed as a series of numbers each representing the number of times that a short sequence was repeated. The strings of numbers could be easily computerized; allowing profiles to be stored, compared and searched." And by 1999, an advanced version of SGM enabled analysis of "even smaller fragments of biological material than SGM."

But as the DNA technology expanded, the defense attorney industry and scholarly skeptics raised doubts. The founding of the DNA Task Force of the National Association of Criminal Defense Attorneys, which grew out of a 1987 murder case that drew attention in the legal community to the use of DNA evidence, brought greater focus to a flaw of this forensic tool.

Joseph Castro was charged with the February 5, 1987 stabbing death in New York City of a 20-year-old woman, who was seven months pregnant, and her 2-year-old daughter. A wristwatch worn by Castro when he was arrested was stained with blood, and DNA analysis of this blood was conducted. While upholding "the general scientific acceptance of the theory underlying DNA identification," the Bronx County Supreme Court ruled that "the DNA identification evidence of inclusion is deemed inadmissible, as a matter of law," according to a court transcript. "The testing laboratory failed in several major respects to use the generally accepted scientific techniques and experiments for obtaining reliable results, within a reasonable degree of scientific certainty."

Even though Castro pleaded guilty to the murder, the court ruling opened a key door to the specter of technical error in the use of such evidence.

"Thanks to cases like this, and to misquoted statements in 1990 by prominent scientists against the use of DNA testing, the courts backed up, allowing the use of DNA to exclude suspects as the source of origin but not to make claims that the suspect's DNA was a match for the collected evidence," wrote Ramsland. "Prosecution experts had to work hard to prove that DNA evidence and analysis could perform as they claimed."

Better methods developed over the ensuing months improved the accuracy of such testing "and strengthened the technology that could demonstrate that the chance a sample matched a particular person showed statistical odds so overwhelming that the courts allowed it for stronger claims," Ramsland wrote. "In 1992, the National Research Council Committee of the National Academy of Sciences affirmed the use of DNA but recommended tight regulations over collection and analysis, and that testing be done by those with no stake in the outcome."

The integrity of the evidence – which would be an issue in the Janet Walsh case – remains a central arguing point in criminal cases involving DNA analysis, and, noted Ramsland, legal challenges "are not limited to the credibility of the lab, human error during evidence collection, or new techniques."

But the growing number of success stories of DNA analysis matching crime victims to suspects overshadowed the lingering doubts.

One such story was the 2000 guilty plea by Jim Stephens to the rape and fatal stabbing in May of 1976 of 18-year-old Kim Kuntz, who was babysitting Melissa, the 3-year-old daughter of her sister, Donna Morris. After Donna returned home shortly before 2 a.m., she could not get into her Snohomish County, Washington, home and called police.

"Inside, Detective John Szalda found Kim dead from repeated stabbing to the chest, and there was also evidence that she had been bound with adhesive and raped," according to Ramsland's account. "Thankfully, Melissa was still alive. Donna asked Melissa if 'Daddy' had come to see her. Melissa nodded, so Donna surmised that her former husband, James Stephens, who had assaulted her just weeks before, had murdered Kim."

Police located Stephens at a Bellingham, Washington motel. His neck and chest were scratched, and he had rug burns on his elbow, "and a patrol officer who spoke to Stephens shortly after the murder remembered seeing a roll of athletic tape in the backseat of Stephens's car. At the crime scene, detectives found semen, and a serology test indicated it might belong to Stephens, but it was from the same bed on which his ex-wife said he had raped her, so it could not be proved that he was a killer. The investigation went cold."

But the evidence was stored, and after the advent of DNA analysis, Detective Jim Rider fetched the T-shirt that Kim was wearing the night of her rape and murder, and he ordered it analyzed, which was done with the use of new light beam technology that would play a prominent role in the Janet Walsh investigation years later.

"If the sample had been properly dried, he knew," Ramsland wrote of Rider, "there was still the possibility of extracting DNA from it." The T-shirt was scanned using various wavelengths of intense light, and analysts "found two or three areas that glowed." An analyst "lifted a sample from the shirt and treated it with a chemical reagent. The chemical reacted with some of the acid phosphate in the semen stains and changed the color of the sample area. A second test further defined the area that could possibly contain semen, and he managed to extract a DNA profile. Police got a warrant for a sample of Jim Stephens's blood, and within six weeks, they had a match. He pleaded guilty to murder and was sentenced to a maximum term of thirty-five years."

Another useful development in the use of DNA forensics in crime-solving was the creation in the 1990s of a national Combined DNA Index

System – CODIS – which helped solve another decades-long case, that of the so-called "ski- mask rapist" of North Carolina.

Jerry Lee Brooks was an unlikely serial rapist. A bank executive who had done prison time after being convicted of stealing millions of dollars from financial institutions in North and South Carolina, Brooks had "spun a story" for FBI agents when he was first interviewed about the thefts, according to a February 2013 article in Charlotte Magazine. Brooks told the agents "he was at work early one day when someone came into his bank with a note saying a bomb would detonate if he didn't hand over the money. Brooks ended up serving time over the past three decades for a variety of offenses, including armed robbery. He was released from federal prison in 2005."

But it was no bank honcho that Mindy Sypher remembers from the night of September 21, 1979. She told the magazine about seeing the mug shot of Brooks on an evening news program in July of 2012 reporting on the case of the "ski-mask rapist."

"The 53-year-old says she remembers every detail of the last time she saw those eyes, on September 21, 1979," the magazine reported. "Sitting in her living room now she barely hesitates as she relays them. The man in the ski mask who had broken into her home. His neatly trimmed fingernails, crisp shirt, and matching tennis whites. The purple dress she wore. His threats that he would cut her.

"Watching the news that July evening, she knew nothing of the life of the man who she says raped her, the 10 other Charlotte women police believe he assaulted, or how he got caught. All she knew was that she believed she was looking at the man she holds responsible for the worst day of her life, and until that moment, she thought he had gotten away with it."

The mother of two told the magazine that Brooks had raped her when she was a 20-year-old theater major at UNCC.

"The media had been reporting on the serial rapist for months," the magazine reported. "Random attacks were rare, and serial rapists were almost unheard of, so the story was getting a lot of play in the newspaper. Sypher still has the yellowed newspaper clipping that tells her story.

"It was a warm September day, and Sypher wore a thin purple dress," the article continued. When she entered the house, "she could see a sliver of light coming from the front door. She thought she'd accidentally left it open. She reached to shut it and bolt the lock when a man jumped out from the bathroom just off the foyer. He grabbed her from behind and she noticed his perfectly manicured hands. She looked down and saw pristine white tennis shoes. His face was covered with a mask, only his eyes and lips visible. Stunned, her first thought was that it was a friend playing a joke. The shoes and the nails didn't fit her mental image of a rapist.

"Her attacker told her he was there to rob her, but Sypher knew instinctively he'd come for something else. The clean-cut man she guessed was about her age threatened to cut her if she didn't perform oral sex. He straddled her. He raped her. He wore the ski mask the whole time."

Sypher's case went cold, but Detective Troy Armstrong of the Charlotte-Mecklenburg

Police Department's sexual assault cold case unit stayed with it, analyzing her case along with the 1981 rape of a pregnant woman in her home. This was a time before DNA analysis, so the evidence sat in storage. Then, in 2006, police department technicians uploaded DNA from the pregnant woman's case to CODIS. "Another four years passed before CODIS matched that DNA to a suspect. (In 2010 the feds uploaded thousands of DNA profiles into the system, taking samples from felons as their prison times ended.) Armstrong was thrilled when he finally got a hit that led to a suspect, a man named Roger Dale Honeycutt. He had been in federal prison for a sex crime involving a young girl, and his DNA was part of the massive 2010 upload."

According to lab results, two serial rapists had been preying on women in Charlotte in the late 1970s and early 1980s. Some of the DNA matched Honeycutt's (who in February of 2013 was convicted of raping two Charlotte women and sentenced to 60 years), "but the rest belonged to someone else, an unknown."

Then, CODIS turned up another suspect.

"Armstrong grins when remembering the day in April 2012 they got a note from the lab saying there had been a hit. Finally, they had a name: Jerry Lee Brooks.

"He was in the system because he was a convicted bank robber," Armstrong told the magazine. Police arrested the 62-year-old Brooks outside of his Surfside Beach, South Carolina, townhouse and charged him with three counts of rape, two counts of crimes against nature, burglary, two counts of breaking and entering, robbery with a dangerous weapon, and two counts of kidnapping.

In November of 2013, Brooks, thanks to the evidence provided by CODIS, pleaded guilty to three counts of first-degree rape and was sentenced to life in prison.

The computerized national CODIS database was created by Congress in 1994 with passage of the DNA Identification Act, spurred in part by a 1990 report by the congressional Office of Technology Assessment (OTA). The OTA, citing the use of DNA testing in more than 2,000 criminal investigations in 49 states to provide evidence in more than 185 court cases, concluded that while "the principles of DNA identification 'are solid' and that 'forensic uses of DNA tests are both reliable and valid when properly performed and analyzed by skilled personnel,' " national standards needed to be established, according to an Associated Press account of the report. "Law enforcement agencies, particularly the FBI, want to establish a data bank of DNA markers, similar to the national files of fingerprints, to help in the investigation of crime," the Associated Press reported.

The DNA Identification Act enabled the FBI to create the CODIS, "containing the DNA profiles contributed by federal, state, and local participating forensic laboratories," according to the fact sheet on the FBI Laboratory Services website.

The FBI launched a component of CODIS known as the National DNA Index System (NDIS) in 1998, wrote Ramsland. The NDIS was the CODIS "capstone," she wrote, "which uses a multilevel software package designed to facilitate computerized cross-checks. All states have profile databases of specific types of convicted felons, and the FBI's CODIS is a vast DNA profile index to which participating labs can submit samples for electronic comparison … During its initial experimental phase over a three-year period, the FBI used CODIS to link nearly two hundred crime scenes to felons."

Meanwhile, the national press was paying increasing attention to DNA as an investigative and evidentiary tool in criminal cases. A November 1998 issue of Newsweek noted that thousands of suspects had been convicted since the seminal Pitchfork case thanks to "DNA's near-miraculous ability to search out suspects across space and time."

The magazine noted several prominent investigations abetted by DNA analysis.

"The long arm of DNA investigation reached into history to implicate Thomas Jefferson in an extramarital affair with a slave," reported the magazine, "helped identify the remains of the last Russian tsar and his family and sealed the case that President Clinton was the source of the world's most famous dress stain. DNA evidence was central to the murder case against O.J. Simpson – and the case collapsed, in part, when defense attorney Barry Sheck showed how the police mishandled the crucial blood drops. The power of DNA evidence will increase enormously in the next few years as the FBI adds millions of samples to the national DNA database that went into operation last month – and so, of course, will the concerns of civil libertarians."

For the time being, the magazine observed, DNA remained a tool basically used for identification. "For that purpose, it's ideal: unique to an individual (except in the case of identical twins); unchanging throughout life; found in cells from skin, blood, hair follicles (although not the shaft), blood, saliva and semen. Technicians can obtain a usable quantity of DNA from the saliva on a cigarette butt or a single hair root. The 'short-tandem-repeat' method used by the FBI to analyze DNA takes measurements in 13 separate places and can match two samples with a theoretical error rate of less than one in a trillion."

Thus, DNA has joined the company of fingerprinting and other biological elements in which it is present – blood types, hair follicles, saliva, semen, tissue, or urine – to provide a method of scientific identification that, according to the U.S. Department of Justice's National Institute of Justice, as of the 2004 publication date of Ramsland's book, "has had an intensity of scrutiny far greater than other methods of criminal investigation … The scientific foundations of DNA are solid."

Even more solid than fingerprints, which used to be the gold standard of evidence in courtrooms – "and that's how the FBI wants people to think of DNA, as a simple aid to identification," according to the Newsweek analysis.

So, DNA forensics had by the second decade of the 21st century evolved quite a ways from its origins. The rapid development during the years that coincided with the Walsh murder would ultimately open the ensuing investigative dead ends of that case. The elements, methods and issues of the development of DNA in crime-fighting – surreptitious gathering of a DNA sample, testing of multiple suspect samples, the potential for evidence tampering or deterioration, analysis using light technology – all would be there as law enforcement officials began to reinvestigate the 1979 murder.

5

Pennsylvania State Trooper Rocco De-
Maiolo remembers his knees buckling when he
got word that semen had been found on clothing
and bed items stored from the Janet Walsh murder scene. Evidence in the Walsh case, kept all
these years in state police facilities, had been gone
over again and again since the late 1990s, when
it was given to the Greensburg Regional Crime
Laboratory in 2010 for analysis.

"I have to be honest," DeMaiolo, the latest
trooper to inherit the Walsh investigation, would
testify in court three years later, "having it for fifteen years and feeling that there was nothing on
there, I, I wasn't confident that they would find
anything. I just wanted to make sure that every
avenue had been crossed in this case."

And so, when he heard from Ashlee Mangan of the state police crime lab that something was found, "it was pretty exciting," he said. "Ashlee called me up, and that's the only time in my life my knees buckled because I was standing up at my desk when she said, 'we found semen,' and that, that caught me off guard, and then when she said that it wasn't just, like, one little spot here, she explained that they found it on the bed sheets, they found it on the back of the nightie, that they found it on the rope or bathrobe rope that was tying her hands, that was just hugely significant to me."

Indeed, it was significant to all of the investigators, including Detective Andrew Gall, who had pushed the troopers to take the Walsh evidence to the lab for DNA analysis. Armed with this newly obtained scientific evidence, Gall and his state police colleagues went back to the primary suspects seeking their DNA to compare to the samples found on the bedding, nightgown and the robe cord used to bind Janet's hands behind her back.

"When we received the news on the DNA, the state police chose to run Scott Walsh first,"

Gall would remember during an interview in the summer of 2014. "We had a copy of (Carlo's) DNA from the Prince Georges County/Whittier investigation, and it did not match." Neither did a sample that Gall later obtained from Carlo voluntarily.

Gall told DeMaiolo that Walsh would volunteer his DNA "without hesitation. Roc said he wanted a search warrant in his pocket in case he refused. We wrote and obtained a sealed warrant from Judge Richard Mancini and called Scott into the state police station.

"I re-interviewed Scott and asked for the DNA sample, and he started to roll up his sleeves to give blood. We told him it was just a swab, and he gave it voluntarily. We did not serve the warrant." Walsh's DNA did not match the DNA found on the cord, bedding and nightgown.

Next on this list of suspects to be sampled was Janet Walsh's employer, Ron Ciccozzi. Again, Gall told DeMaiolo that no warrant would be necessary; but they had one, just in case. Ciccozzi was tested voluntarily, and again, there was no match.

Gall went to Massachusetts to obtain a sample of McGrail's DNA. He coordinated with Trooper Josh Ulrich of the Massachusetts State Police, and Ulrich obtained a search warrant.

"When we picked up McGrail, I started to talk to him about a DNA sample," Gall said. "He was considering it but had not yet agreed when Trooper Ulrich served him with the warrant. Even then, McGrail said we did not need it and that he would give it voluntarily, but we went through the legal route." There was no match.

The elimination of four of the original five suspects left Gregory Scott Hopkins.

"I felt he would not be willing to give a DNA sample. We could not develop enough probable cause for a search warrant," Gall recalled. And Hopkins was adept at leaving no trace of DNA during the interview process.

"We called for him but had to leave messages, and he did not return the first couple," Gall said. "He finally called me back and agreed to meet at the state police station. He refused a cup of coffee and brought his own water bottle. He took the empty bottle with him when he left. He claimed he barely remembered Janet Walsh and did not recall any specific sexual contact with her. When I asked him for a DNA sample he refused immediately, saying that he did not want it on some national database for everyone to access. I assured him that we would only use it for comparison on this case. He said it was his right to refuse. I waited and called him again a few weeks later. He again refused. I received a letter from his attorney stating that we are to leave him alone. I got a letter from the DA and the manager of the crime lab saying that it would only be used for comparison in this case then destroyed. Again, they refused."

So Gall tried another avenue, which would require the assistance of the police force in Bridgewater, a small town of about 700 where Hopkins was a councilman and regularly visited borough headquarters. The online BeaverCountian.com reported on February 5, 2012, how Gall and Bridgewater Police Chief Doug Adams collaborated to obtain a sample of Hopkins' DNA.

"Detective Andrew Gall contacted Bridgewater Police to inquire about the town's garbage pickup schedule," the BeaverCountian.com reported. "Gall was planning to gather trash placed out for pickup by Hopkins, in hopes of finding a possible DNA sample. It was then that Chief Adams suggested a different approach.

"As a Councilman with the borough, Hopkins would regularly visit the Borough Building, and often would have a drink of water while there, using a Styrofoam cup he would then throw away. Chief Adams told Detective Gall he believed a sample could be obtained of Hopkins from the cup."

In August of 2011, Hopkins visited the borough building and had a cup of water, which Adams took from the trash and gave to Gall later the same day. The cup "was transported to a State Crime Lab in Greensburg for testing," the news site reported. "Police say the results of that preliminary testing showed Gregory Scott Hopkins could not be eliminated as a potential suspect in the Walsh murder, based on DNA found in semen gathered from a nightgown and rope collected at the crime scene in 1979.

"In December of last year," the article continued, "investigators took that preliminary analysis before a Beaver County Judge. That judge determined the testing provided enough probable cause to grant a search warrant, compelling Gregory Hopkins to turn over a DNA sample."

The analysis of that sample turned up a match to the evidence items, and on Sunday, January 29, 2012, police arrested Hopkins, as recounted January 30 in the BeaverCountian.com.

"Some 33 years ago, Pete Caltury was sitting in his living room with police and detectives. He had just finished serving them all a slice of pie, as they began to tell him the investigation into the murder of his twenty-three year old daughter, Catherine Walsh, had stalled," the news site reported. "Yesterday, Pete was once again serving slices of pie to law enforcement. They had come to his home to inform him the man they believed killed his child was under arrest. It was news that the girl's mother, who died 7 years ago, would never hear.

"Bridgewater Councilman Gregory Scott Hopkins, 65, of 718 Mulberry Street, Bridgewater, was charged Sunday in connection with Walsh's murder."

The Pittsburgh Post-Gazette also put an historical frame on the arrest story, pointing out that the Walsh case was Gall's "first homicide, and for 32 years it went unsolved. 'This is the first one, and it was always the one that bothered me,' he said. Over the years, Detective Gall, now the assistant chief county detective in the Beaver County district attorney's office, stayed in contact with Mr. Caltury. He kept case reports in his desk and drove his wife crazy puzzling over the case as it grew cold.

"On Monday, Detective Gall, now 57, stood beside Beaver County District Attorney Anthony J. Berosh as Mr. Berosh announced that Gregory S. Hopkins, 65, had been charged with criminal homicide in the 1979 death of Mrs. Walsh."

The newspaper reported that Hopkins, who owned a construction and snow removal business in Bridgewater, had been arraigned the previous Sunday night and was being held without bond in the Beaver County jail. In the ensuing weeks, the press pieced together a profile of

Hopkins and of his community and its residents – some of whom expressed shock and surprise over his arrest.

A Pittsburgh Post-Gazette piece published February 1, 2012, depicted Bridgewater, located near the confluence of the Beaver and Ohio rivers, as "the kind of small town where neighbors help each other protect their homes before it floods."

Scott Jeffers told the newspaper he had met Hopkins a couple of years before when residents gathered to construct a small home for a man who had been paralyzed. Jeffers said he was "shocked" to hear of the criminal homicide charge brought against Hopkins. " 'I have never seen him raise his temper to anybody,' " Jeffers told the newspaper.

"In Pit-Stop and throughout the town, shock was a common reaction among Bridgewater residents, although many declined to give their names or speak further," the newspaper reported. "Bridgewater residents could shed little light on Mr. Hopkins, who was appointed councilman about two years ago and elected last fall to a four-year term that began this month.

"On Bridgewater's website, Mr. Hopkins appears frequently in the minutes of council meetings, often reading aloud the finance report.

" 'He is a nice guy,' said William Rains, vice president of the council. 'He helped us through the budget.'

"Mr. Rains, who said he did not know Mr. Hopkins well outside of council business, said he believed he was married, with grown children. He did not know how long Mr. Hopkins had lived in Bridgewater, which is less than a 10-minute drive from Monaca."

***

On February 3, the BeaverCountian.com published a piece that Hopkins and his attorney, James Ross of Ambridge, certainly would not welcome: a scathing indictment of Hopkins' relationship with his first wife, based on transcripts of the April 19, 1979 divorce proceeding brought by her, which, according to the article, "detailed a troubled marriage marred by infidelity."

The hearing came before Anthony Berosh,

then a master – a Beaver County judicial officer – who would be the county's district attorney and Andrew Gall's boss when Hopkins was arrested.

According to the transcript, Hopkins' then-wife "testified problems began just a couple years into their marriage. He would be gone a lot; 'he would go out after dinner and play pool with the guys and come home like two or three in the morning, but, you know, that wasn't anything major at the time,' she said.

"But according to her, those problems grew more pronounced as time passed. 'When I was in labor with my first child, he left to go on an appointment and left me at home with my mother, who doesn't drive, and said if anything develops to call the police and they would take me to the hospital,' she testified, describing Gregory as having 'a total lack of consideration and caring of what happened to me.' "

Hopkins would ignore her at parties, she testified.

" 'He would pay attention to everyone else and fool around with them like I wasn't there; and through the years, it got more pronounced. I was highly embarrassed that I was left alone sitting and he would be getting up and dancing and I would be sitting there by myself.' "

In April of 1977, she learned that she was pregnant with the couple's third child, and later that same year Hopkins confessed to her that he was having an affair. The couple was hosting an open house at their home, and she had been working to prepare, she said, when Hopkins told her of his affair.

" 'He said, "I have to talk to you," and he says, "I have been seeing someone. I just wanted you to know because her husband found out and he said he is coming to the party tomorrow and telling you about it in front of everyone here. He is also in the real estate field," and it was awful; I don't know how I got through that party the next day. I stayed, and every time you would walk in the room, I felt everybody was talking about it. It was awful. At the time, I was about five or six months pregnant. It was terrible.' "

That affair continued, she testified, along with others – " 'I was stopped at a place to have lunch coming home from the obstetrician, and my husband and another girl pulled in at the same place for lunch, and I was totally embarrassed.' "

The divorce became final in June of 1980.

At a bail hearing the same day that the BeaverCountian.com piece was published, Common Pleas Judge Mancini denied a bail request by Hopkins, who wore a neatly trimmed, closely cropped gray beard and eyeglasses beneath a bald head and a prison uniform with wide, horizontal stripes. He was handcuffed and his legs shackled. Karen Hopkins, his wife since 2001, "sat in the row behind him with four other people," the Post-Gazette reported on February 4. Ross "argued that prosecutors do not have evidence of premeditation, what he called 'the key' in a first-degree murder case.

"The evidence in Mrs. Walsh's bedroom, which had no signs of a struggle, could be a 'sexual encounter gone bad,' " argued Hopkins' attorney, signaling what might be a defense ploy during trial of presenting the events the morning of Walsh's death as kinky sex gone awry. " 'At best,' " Ross argued, " 'this could rise to the level of third-degree murder,' a low enough count that it would not carry a life sentence and therefore would allow bail to be granted, he said.

"Judge Richard Mancini ruled there was sufficient evidence (that) the case involved a non-bailable offense and ordered Mr. Hopkins back to jail."

Hopkins had been through multiple marriages, according to the Post-Gazette's background investigation. His first marriage, in 1967, "ended in divorce in 1980. Mr. Hopkins married again in 1983 and divorced in 1999. He married Karen L. Fisher, his current wife, in 2001."

After bond was denied, the Associated Press on February 4 did a situationer on the case, offering some context and mood to what had been to date a basic crime story.

"As a small town comes to grips with a 32-year-old murder, the talk isn't just about a borough councilman being held without bond in a local jail," began the piece. "The long-forgotten murder of 23-year-old Catherine Walsh has also brought back memories of a man who may have been unjustly accused, as residents ponder the difference between reputation and true character."

Murder had not frequently visited Monaca or the nearby communities, a region Rudyard Kipling had described as a " 'peaceful, placid Beaver and its boundless cordiality, its simple, genuine hospitality,' " the AP reported. "There was none in Monaca Borough last year and just five robberies, according to state crime statistics. There wasn't a single robbery or murder in Bridgewater, and Beaver borough had just one robbery."

The article proceeded to round out the character of Hopkins, who grew up on the same street as Dave Porter, who told the AP that he had for many years played hockey with Scott Walsh, Janet's estranged husband.

When news of Hopkins' arrest "began to filter through the community, Porter said most people were stunned. And if Hopkins had a known flaw, it was hardly a criminal one," according to the AP account. " 'He had an edge to him, but the edge was he liked profit, he liked money,' Porter said. Public records show that in 2006 a building company sued Hopkins, who owned a construction company. The building company recovered a $52,654 judgment for unpaid bills and legal fees."

Checking with residents around town, the AP reporter found some folks unwilling to talk about Hopkins and the case.

"A man at one downtown bar said he knew Hopkins but then declined to speak after the bartender motioned with her hands. Others froze at just the mention of Hopkins' name."

Such reactions, suggested Pittsburgh's Duquesne University law Professor Bruce Ledewitz, might be caused by residents' struggle with reconciling "the allegations of murder with a man they thought they knew."

" 'People who were murderers don't always act like murderers,' as time goes on, Ledewitz said. 'It's like the cases in which a radical blows up a building in the '60s, and then goes underground and becomes a regular citizen.' He added that many details about the case against Hopkins are still not public."

Ledewitz raised one issue that defense attorney Ross would seize upon in the ensuing trial.

"Ledewitz said the details of the evidence

will be crucial if the case goes to trial," the AP reported. "For example, he said, 'semen is not necessarily evidence that the person who had sex with her killed her. Then all you have is that he had sex with her around that time.' "

And the article closed with an ominous air, so far as Ross and Hopkins would be concerned:

"Ledewitz said a person's reputation in a community can make a difference in a possible trial.

" 'But police don't care how good a life you've led,' he said. 'In this case, I think the community will eventually wake up.' "

***

On March 29, 2012, Magisterial District Judge Joseph Schafer bound the case over to trial at the preliminary hearing, at which Ross previewed another possible defense tactic after informing the court that his client pleaded not-guilty to the charges, the Post-Gazette reported March 30, 2012.

"Given that Mr. Hopkins had previously had a sexual relationship with Ms. Walsh, Mr. Ross called it a 'quantum leap' to say that the presence of his DNA meant he was responsible for her death," the newspaper reported, as Ross then raised the possibility of tainted DNA evidence. "He also questioned if anyone knew how often Ms. Walsh had washed her clothing and bed sheets. 'It is not an earth-shattering announcement that his DNA is there,' Mr. Ross said. 'It should be there.' " This, because Hopkins had admitted, during his original questioning by police, to having sexual relations with Janet Walsh.

"Yet oral and vaginal swabs performed on Janet had yielded no DNA match with Hopkins, Mr. Ross said. Frank Martocci, assistant district attorney, said Ms. Walsh's DNA profile was the only other one identified at the scene."

During his questioning of Richard Matas, a retired state police trooper who was among the first responders to the murder scene, Ross tested the legal waters that he might swim during the defense portion of the trial to come. Ross suggested, as he had at the bail hearing, that the killing may have begun as a sexual escapade gone bad.

The retired state trooper testified that this possibility had been entertained during the investigation, and that near-choking can enhance a sexual climax. Such a "scenario," he said, "was possible."

The officer, who collected the bandana, the bath robe tie, the nightie and a dress on an ironing table for evidence, said he did not ask that the bandana be dusted for fingerprints. Such technology was not available then, he testified. It was not in the realm of possibility then to test a bandana for fingerprints.

But the testimony of Janet Walsh's 90-year-old father dominated the preliminary hearing.

Caltury recounted the now-familiar story of finding his daughter dead in her apartment the morning of September 1, 1979. The house was clean, with no sign of struggle, Matas and Caltury testified before a packed court proceeding, which had to be moved from the originally scheduled courtroom because of an overflow audience of more than 50 observers.

Wearing a red-and-white plaid shirt

beneath a gray Cardigan sweater, the slightly balding, thin, bespeckled father said that on the day he discovered the body, he went to visit his daughter at the Indiana Avenue rental property owned by his mother, where his daughter rented the main-floor apartment in a house that had been converted into two apartments. He and his wife, Mary Jane, went to the house, Caltury testified. He went into the house screaming out her name, he said, then went to her bedroom.

"I saw her in bed, face down," he testified. He pulled down the cover, saw that her hands were tied behind her back. Sipping from a cup of water provided by the judge, he testified lucidly that he felt his daughter's pulse and determined she was dead.

In response to questioning from Ross, Caltury testified that he noticed nothing out of sorts in the house.

The defense attorney read from a statement taken at the time indicating that Caltury thought his daughter's ex-husband, Scott Walsh, was "bitter" towards her, but Caltury could not recall saying that.

Justice Delayed

"They were already divorced."

Ross reminded Caltury that he had reported the ex-husband driving by the house, but Caltury could not recall if he had seen Scott Walsh, or if he had been told that Scott had driven by.

Ross wondered if Caltury knew how often his daughter did the laundry, and if she had a washer and dryer in the house. Caltury, in what would be his last public utterance concerning the case of his murdered daughter, said he did not know. A year and three months later, on June 28, 2013, Caltury died at Rochester Manor.

His obituary identified him as a 1938 graduate of Monaca High School, a World War II Marine veteran, member of the St. John the Baptist Catholic Church in Monaca, and a graduate of Robert Morris Business School who had worked at Pittsburgh Tool & Steel and at Westinghouse Electric in Vanport before retiring as a senior purchasing agent at H.H. Robertson in Ambridge. He was preceded in death by his wife and two sons, John, who died as an infant, and Peter Joseph, who had died in 2011 – and, of course, by Catherine Janet Walsh.

The case was to go to trial in November of 2012 but was suspended after Common Pleas Judge Harry E. Knafelc ruled on November 5 that testimony planned by forensic pathologist Cryil H. Wecht, a renowned former coroner for neighboring Allegheny County, was inadmissible "because it lacked scientific basis" according to a December 4 Pittsburgh Post-Gazette account. The district attorney's office on November 14 appealed that decision to the state Superior Court, and Ross asked for a bail hearing "saying that the pending appeal could keep his client in the Beaver County Jail for another year, infringing on Mr. Hopkins' right to a speedy trial." On Monday, December 3, Knafelc granted bond to Hopkins, who was released from jail.

The testimony from Wecht would be damning, if allowed. The prosecution case "hinged on the DNA evidence found in seminal fluid left on the back of Walsh's nightgown, on the rope tied around her hands and the bed sheet that covered her body," the Pittsburgh Post-Gazette had reported on November 20. "According to court documents," the newspaper reported,

"Dr. Wecht's report states that the fact that the DNA was found only on the bed sheet, the back of Walsh's nightgown and on the rope around her wrists makes it 'extremely unlikely' that the DNA was left during earlier sexual encounters with Walsh. Dr. Wecht also argues in his report that the location of the DNA places Mr. Hopkins on the bed on top of Walsh at or around the time of her death, and he gives his opinion that she died due to 'strangulation during sexual activity.' "

Despite Knafelc's finding that Wecht's conclusions "were 'too vague and imprecise' and were 'speculative in nature,' " the state Superior Court ruled the Wecht testimony and report admissible nearly a year later, according to the newspaper account. The report on the DNA evidence "meets Pennsylvania's liberal standard for expert testimony and should not have been precluded," Superior Court Judge John L. Musmanno wrote for the majority.

The ruling, while disappointing to Ross, would not change his strategy, he told the newspaper.

"Mr. Ross has argued repeatedly that because the two Beaver County residents were having an affair, Mr. Hopkins' DNA should be in the apartment," reported the newspaper.

That would be but one of the arguments put forth by Ross when the case finally went to trial on November 12, 2013.

Indeed, DNA would be the central issue in the opening arguments of the prosecution and defense – along with character and credibility issues that would evolve more fully during the trial.

One of the character issues – that of Hopkins' relationship with and treatment of women – was brought to the fore symbolically by District Attorney Anthony Berosh in his decision to have the female half of his prosecuting team, Assistant District Attorney Brittany Smith, present the opening statement of the trial to the five-man, seven-woman jury. Smith knew the geographical terrain of the case well, growing up in Beaver County's Hopewell Township, where she now lives, and graduating from Hopewell High in 1999 before earning her bachelor's at Penn State and earning her law degree in 2006 from Duquesne University in Pittsburgh. Berosh hired her immediately upon her graduation from Duquesne.

After first recapping the discovery of Janet Walsh's body by her parents and the arrival of police officers to the scene of the murder, Smith focused on what would be the crucial scientific evidence of the trial.

"Now, at this time in 1979, DNA was not a thought," Smith told the jurors, reminding them of the changing technology over the long period of time that had elapsed since the 1979 murder. She quickly summarized the prosecution's argument for the validity of the DNA samples and evidence.

"Nobody knew that DNA was even on the horizon. But the state police gather up the evidence. They package it carefully. They log it into evidence and preserve it, and there it sits."

Smith recapped for the jurors the events of the evening before the discovery of the body – the visits by Janet Walsh and her friends to the bars, the dancing and conviviality, the early morning meal at Perkins; and in a tactical maneuver for the prosecution to be the first to bring into the court record the other suspects that prosecutors knew would be questioned by Ross, she introduced the jurors to their names: Scott Walsh, Robert Mc-Grail, Ron Ciccozzi and Carlo.

"And you will also hear that through the investigation, there was nothing to tie them to the crime scene either.

"Obviously, her estranged husband is also a suspect. So, they questioned his whereabouts that night, and Scott Walsh will tell you, ladies and gentlemen, what he was doing that Friday night," she said, carefully moving the jury toward the entry of Scott Hopkins into the case and his secret love affair with Janet Walsh – and in the process casting a negative character light, his womanizing, on the defendant.

"Nobody else knows about this relationship," Smith told the jurors. "Scott Hopkins was married and estranged from his wife, Ellen, and was seeing another woman, Dianne St. George, and he's seeing Dianne St. George at the time that he's having the relationship with Janet Walsh."

Smith then raised what would be a key issue in the trial, Hopkins' credibility.

"Pay close attention to what he tells Detective Gall and the other investigators because, at first, he says that he doesn't really know her. He knows her to see her, and then he finally admits that he has a sexual relationship with her; he's been there a couple of times, two, maybe one, and the last time he was there was three or four weeks prior to the incident."

Back to the DNA, Smith summarized for the jurors the strength of that evidence.

"The serology expert from the Pennsylvania State Police Crime Lab gives a rating to seminal stains," she said, "one-plus meaning there's just a little bit there, to four-plus; that's the highest rating they give. The rating on those areas I told you about, the rope, nightgown, top sheet? Four-plus for the defendant."

Finally, Smith invoked the name of Dr. Cyril Wecht, well-known in Western Pennsylvania because of the doctor's long and distinguished background as an Allegheny County coroner and an established expert in forensics that included DNA analysis.

"Dr. Cyril Wecht will testify," she told the jurors, "and he will tell you that (the semen) was deposited around the time of her death" – a key finding, as Smith anticipated that defense attorney Ross would question the time element of the semen deposits.

Ross, participating in his last major criminal trial before taking seat as a new judge (elected that very month) of the Court of Common Pleas of Beaver County, went straight to the DNA in his opening statement. The strategy was intended to make a strength of what the prosecution portrayed as a defense weakness.

"Let's get something out of the way right away," he told the jurors. "We're not contesting that my client's DNA was at the scene. We're not contesting that it was on the back of the nightgown; we're not contesting that it was on the robe tie."

Raising the possibility of tainted or misinterpreted DNA evidence, Ross told the jurors that he wanted them to believe that Hopkins' DNA was there, "because I'm going to tell you this: As this case goes on, I encourage you to consider that evidence because this case will show an abuse of the use of DNA in a case, and that DNA will actually become favorable and exculpatory to my client."

Ross posed to the jury questions of whether the DNA evidence was properly sealed, of the possibility of transfer of DNA from one item to another by officers and lab technicians, of why Hopkins' DNA was not found in other locations where it might logically be expected to appear, of why the DNA evidence found in sperm that had been there for more than three decades would on the one hand indicate sexual activity when the state laboratory report "says there was no evidence of recent sexual activity" – along with the lack of spermal DNA evidence inside the body of Janet Walsh.

Ross then cited what would become a key focus of the defense concerning the DNA evidence: the finding of "no visible trace evidence" on the blue bandana used to strangle the young woman, "and you will hear from Trooper De-Maiolo that he submitted this evidence, the ligature, in 2005 because it was the best, and I quote that, the best evidence from which they could obtain trace evidence of who did this, and there's no

DNA found on that ligature."

The rape kit, Ross told the jurors, "did not contain any evidence in 1979 that there had been any sexual activity based on the tests that they did."

Conceding that the relationship between Hopkins and Walsh had become one in which both "just sought sex," Ross said there had been not just two, but "several evenings during that summer, either Miss Walsh would call Hopkins or Hopkins would call Walsh, and the two would get together for sex only. Mr. Hopkins had sex in the very bed where Janet Walsh was found. We're not denying that. We're not disputing that. He told the police this in 1979. He told them that, and he was not a suspect until 2011. Gregory Scott Hopkins' semen was deposited in that location. It should be there. It was there."

Ross then discussed his version of the suspect list, raising questions particularly about McGrail and Scott Walsh – the latter engaging "in some very suspicious conduct on the morning of September first" – and pointing out that Hopkins had three alibi witnesses for his whereabouts at the time of the murder and a reputation for community service and as a successful businessman.

"He has no criminal record," Ross said of Hopkins. "Thirty-four years have passed, many things have happened, but not once will you hear that my client ever made any admission of guilt to anyone about this incident. No witness has ever come forward to place him at the scene."

As for that problematic DNA, Ross told the jurors, it would be less troublesome in light of the age of the DNA samples along with other questions that included the investigating officers' failure to test a robe found in Janet Walsh's apartment that carried the DNA of an unknown person, and the findings of Scott Walsh's DNA on the bed sheets.

Plus, to rebut Wecht, the defense team of Ross and his colleague, Charles F. Bowers III, planned to call upon a DNA expert who was a participant and a member of the board of the Cyril Wecht Institute and wrote a chapter on DNA for a book on forensic science for lawyers edited by Wecht. Ross' expert also had taken DNA forensics to a new technical level by using computer technology to produce statistical analyses of DNA evidence.

Ross summed up for jurors what he considered to be the scientific gist of the case.

"I suggest to you," he told the jurors, "that this case will be a classroom for you in DNA. It will be fascinating, but what you will learn is this: No one can determine how or when DNA is deposited on an item. The only thing that can be determined is that it's there. It can come from direct contact, from someone touching you, and that's what the state police were looking for on the bandana in 2005."

DNA can be transferred from one item to another, Ross told the jurors, and it "can be transferred into the wash. It can be carried to one item from another by liquid … You're going to learn that DNA has so many ways to be deposited that it's just astounding."

So, jurors were headed into a sea of testimony that included numerous questions of credibility involving not only technical and scientific issues surrounding a relatively new forensic tool but also age-old matters of personal traits and character, which the prosecuting team would try to explore with its first three witnesses.

But the "fog of time," words invoked by the Pittsburgh Post-Gazette in its coverage of the trial, would make it difficult for the prosecution to recreate the events of the evening before Janet Walsh's murder. And the character and personality of the young woman who was estranged from her husband and high school sweetheart at the time of her death would be explored as the prosecution called its first witnesses to the stand.

6

Like many residents of Monaca then and now, it was a close-knit group of young women who went out for drinks that Friday night before Janet Walsh's murder. Elaine Deluco had known Janet as a young girl because Janet's grandmother lived across the street from Elaine's childhood home. Like Janet, Elaine was a graduate of Monaca High School. She was a sister-in-law of Margie Farinacci, Janet's next-door neighbor during Janet's marriage to Scott Walsh.

She testified in response to questioning by Brittany Smith that she and another sister-in-law of Margie, Georgina (last name Beightley at that time), met up with Margie and Janet at the Getaway bar in the Gee Bee Plaza late in the evening, nearly 11 p.m., after Elaine had put her children to bed. She testified that she also knew Scott Walsh, who had lived across the street from her in-laws.

"The Getaway was crowded that night," she said, and the mood of the four women was simply "to enjoy the evening." The four were "just talking and laughing," she said, "and we all seemed to be just happy to be out." Janet and Georgina, she said, had danced with somebody, but she couldn't recall whom. The women closed the bar. She and Georgina left around 2 or 2:30 a.m., and Janet and Margie went to Perkins for a bite to eat.

The next day, she got a call from Margie who told her that Janet's parents had phoned looking for their daughter, who hadn't shown up for work. Elaine lived around the corner from Janet's apartment, so "I went around the corner, but by then, the police had already been there."

Ross, in his cross-examination, began to sow the seeds of suspicion regarding other suspects.

After establishing that Elaine did not know Hopkins and had not seen him at the bar that night, he elicited testimony from the witness – who relied on her statement to police to refresh her dim memory of that evening – that she had seen Janet dance with a man and that the man had accompanied Janet and Margie to Perkins. And, in a nod to the passage of time, Ross established that no such technology as cell phones and texting existed – and Elaine had not seen Janet Walsh leave the table to make a phone call.

The testimony from Georgina Wilson (Beightley) was similar. Georgina knew Janet from her brother and Margie's house before going for drinks that Friday night of August 31, which was "really the first time I had ever been with Janet."

She remembered the mood that night as "kind of quiet ... we were just, like, talking back and forth. It was no partying or loudness or anything like that. Just relaxing."

As for dancing, she remembered not herself going to the floor, but "maybe Elaine and Janet, not Elaine, but Margie and Janet may have."

She remembered nothing else unusual or specific about the night. She left with Elaine, and her brother, Joey, phoned her the next day to inform her of Janet's murder.

Assistant District Attorney Frank Martocci took over from Smith to question Margie Farinacci, Janet's friend and former Upper Monaca neighbor. Martocci, who earned his law degree from Thomas M. Cooley Law School in Lansing, Michigan in 1991, joined the district attorney's office the same year as Smith but had several homicide cases on his resume along with twelve years' experience as a public defender in Beaver County before becoming a prosecutor.

Martocci found Farinacci's memory of that evening equally cloudy; but it was during her testimony that the prosecution brought Hopkins' name into the testimony. Margie testified that Hopkins, the owner of Colony Square Builders, had built the Ella Street home in Upper Monaca in which Margie had lived for more than 30 years.

"He's over there," she responded when asked to point out Hopkins. In fact, Hopkins had built the home next door, which Janet and Scott Walsh had purchased, along with two other homes on the street that were finished at the same time, in 1977.

When she learned that Hopkins was looking to hire someone to do heavy construction cleaning, she went to work for Colony Square Builders – work she performed, off-and-on as needed, for about a year.

Margie testified that she and Scott Walsh had grown up across the street from each other, so she already knew him when he and Janet moved in as the second buyers of the house next door. The two couples became friends and went out for dinner together.

"Janet was younger, and she instantly just – she was wonderful to my son, absolutely wonderful with him, and it was almost like, you know, he used to call her 'Aunt Janet.' Um, she loved him very much, and he was very close to her."

Once in a while Janet would come visit Margie on the job, "like, bring me lunch. To do a heavy construction clean, it takes a while, and she would stop by and bring something or, you know, whatever."

Then, after Margie learned that Scott and Janet Walsh were having marital problems and that divorce seemed imminent, Janet moved into the apartment on Indiana Street, and that Friday preceding her death she "just wanted to go out, and you know, just kind of unwind to forget the day and things like that."

Janet, Margie and Margie's son met up late that afternoon at Wendy's for dinner, and Janet and Margie decided to go out that night. Margie contacted Elaine and Georgina, and the four women planned to have a girls' night out – a night that began with Janet and Margie stopping in at the Top of the Mall before meeting Elaine and Georgina at the Getaway about a mile away. Margie did not remember personally dancing, but, she testified, all of the women were drinking. The purpose of the evening, she said, was to lift Janet's spirits.

"We were just trying to cheer her up. She was going through a divorce. So, I mean, it was just, you know, trying to have fun, a fun evening with her."

Beyond that, she did not remember Janet dancing with anyone before going to Perkins with Janet afterwards. In fact, as reported by the Pittsburgh Post-Gazette in its November 13 edition, other than recalling learning of her friend's death the day after their Friday night off, she struggled to "remember the smaller details – such as what Walsh ate at the restaurant, where her car was parked and exactly what she told the police in the hours after her friend's body was discovered."

Reading over her statement to police helped her to testify to some of the details, though. For example, she could not recall the dancing man mentioned by the other witnesses, Robert McGrail, joining her and Janet at Perkins. But after reading her statement to the police she could testify that McGrail had apparently sat down in the booth with her and Janet, "and it seemed like from the report he was talking more to Janet, and he thought he was going to be able to get a ride home, and she just kind of told him to move to another table. She – obviously, it sounds like she didn't want to be bothered with him."

According to the statement, McGrail left the table, and she and Janet stayed at the restaurant until about 4 a.m. She went home and to bed, planning to attend a Labor Day picnic with her husband for Colony Square Builders' employees the next day.

After learning of Janet's failure to show up for work the next day, she went to Janet's apartment, where she encountered a chaotic scene, for which she demonstrated stronger recall.

"Her younger brother was outside on the stairs," she testified. "And I could see a lot of commotion. There was a lot of people. I don't know who the people were, neighbors, whatever, all standing out on the street. Um, I saw people, like police officers in uniform, and I didn't know what was going on. I think the street was blocked. I walked up to her brother, and I said, 'what's going on?' And he said, 'she's gone.' I said, 'what are you talking about?' He started crying very hard. He grabbed ahold of me and just held me and cried, and he was shaking, and I'm thinking, 'what is going on?' His words still didn't sink into my head. It did at some point. I don't know how long that lasted."

She walked through the apartment with Gall and the other officers.

"The only thing that I saw that didn't look

right to me was in her bedroom," Farinacci told the court. "Well, when we walked through her bedroom, um, she always had her ironing board up in her bedroom. That's just how she left it, and the dress she had worn that night was laid over the, um, ironing board. Um, her shoes were like on the floor normal, and um, her jewelry was laid out on the dresser, and to me, I'm there like, 'no, that's not right. That's just not right.' I mean, you come home, you're throwing stuff around. You don't set it up, you know? And I, I found that odd."

She continued, expressing the mood that had swept through the town that weekend of the murder:

"At that point, everything just became a nightmare. You're numb. You're being told these things happened, and in the town of Monaca decades ago, things like this just didn't happen. I mean, I never even locked my doors to my house. It's not like in today's world where you can't even walk in your yard without locking your door. I mean, it just didn't happen."

The day of the murder, her husband

phoned Scott Hopkins to inform him that he and his wife would not be attending the Labor Day picnic, and why.

Turning to the girls' night out in his cross-examination, Ross elicited from Margie that Janet had downed "four to five" Southern Comfort Manhattans, that she had danced with McGrail, and that McGrail was looking for a ride home from Perkins afterward. Also, Janet had asked McGrail to leave the table "because her husband gets upset when he sees her with other men; isn't that true?" Ross asked.

"That's what the report said," Margie responded.

Ross also got on the record at this point that Janet had not mentioned Hopkins at any time that evening to Margie.

Exploring further the Scott Walsh-Janet Walsh relationship, Ross called on Margie's statement to the police in which she had told the police that Janet had complained of Scott Walsh following her after the separation and that Scott had been repeatedly questioning her about Janet.

Displaying a photo of the Farinacci home

in relation to that of the Walsh house next door, Ross reminded Margie that it was about 4 a.m. and dark outside when she got home. He asked where her lights would shine when she pulled into her driveway.

"The house on the right," she responded.

"And whose house was that?"

"At the time that was Janet and Scott Walsh."

"And who lived there at that time only?"

"Scott Walsh."

After Ross made the point that the flashing headlights could have alerted Scott that Margie was home from the girls' night out, leaving him time and opportunity to go to Janet's apartment, prosecuting attorney Martocci redirected examination to mute this inference. He asked Farinacci if she had "any reason to believe that Scott Walsh would have seen you arrive, or did you have any contact with him when you got home?"

"I did not have any contact with Scott Walsh that night," she replied, after which she was dismissed from the witness stand.

***

Following testimony by Janet Walsh's brother, Francesco Caltieri, who read the transcript of his dead father's pre-trial testimony about finding Janet's body and calling the police, the prosecution turned to establishing the facts and evidence of the murder and crime scene through the testimony of then-Monaca-police-officer Gall, former county Deputy Coroner Harper Simpson, and Beaver County pathologist Dr. Gary Marcus.

***

Gall, recalling that it was his first homicide as a young officer – "I was 25 years old," he testified; "I had a lot more hair; I was a little thinner back then" – said he had been on patrol at the red light at Old Broadhead "ready to turn into Monaca" when he got the call from the dispatcher to report to the Indiana Street apartment belonging to Janet Walsh. The only news of significance then, Gall testified, "was the fact that the Pirates were on their way to the World Series.

"That was the last time they were in the World Series, and we were all watching the Pirate games."

Gall then testified, with the assistance of projected crime-scene photos and town maps, about the events of the discovery of the body by Janet's father, of entering the crime scene and securing the evidence, and of viewing the body. Her sheet was up to her neck, "and I looked at her face. By the way her face looked, you knew she was dead. So, I knew at that point to shut down the crime scene."

That meant, he explained, ensuring that nobody was "walking around contaminating it."

Gall radioed in to the police chief and then the state police, the coroner's office, a photographer to document the scene, the Beaver County detectives – and an ambulance, "already on the way."

During their walk-through, officers found a letter on the floor below the front-door mail slot, with a check rolled up in a key ring, along with junk mail advertising the Dale Carnegie Institute. The check was a support payment from Scott

Walsh to Janet, and the key ring was attached to a tab labeled "Reliable Refrigeration" – Janet's place of employment.

As a picture of the dead woman was projected for the courtroom, Gall described the light blue workman's handkerchief, or bandana, found around her neck, and her nightgown. The bandana, Gall testified, indicating it on the screen, was "tied very tightly … and it was knotted right up here under her hair."

After state police and the others were called in, Gall said, the case was turned over to the state police, which is how such cases were handled then.

"Some towns turned over armed robberies, but most towns turned over at least homicides," Gall explained, "and they decided that the primary investigating agency of this crime was going to be the Pennsylvania State Police, and that I was going to be assigned to assist them to get around town, places they didn't know, finding people, that type of thing."

Gall testified that he and the others began taking statements from witnesses of the previous evening, friends and others. The prosecuting attorney returned to the handling of the crime scene. He asked Gall if he had worn gloves while going through the evidence.

"Nobody wore gloves in 1979 unless it was wintertime and you were trying to keep your hands warm," Gall testified.

In an effort to again divert the jurors' attention away from Hopkins and toward the estranged husband, Ross in his cross-examination discussed the support check and keys dropped by Scott Walsh in the mail slot.

"And the husband allegedly found those keys in his yard, am I right?"

"Yes, at the house that they had lived in together," Gall answered.

"So, that very morning the husband comes by before you get there and drops off these keys and this check?"

"Yes."

Ross wondered if police had taken or checked any evidence in the wastebasket, checked out a discarded tissue on the floor next to it, or checked the bathroom sink for blood evidence.

Gall testified that such questioning should be posed to state police, because he didn't remove any of the evidence for checking.

The remainder of the first day's testimony was used to establish such facts as cause and time of death and other routine evidentiary matters.

***

Former coroner Simpson, after testifying that this was the first homicide in his hometown of Monaca since his childhood, told the court that the estimated time of death was 5 a.m., based on the pathologist's examination of the contents of Janet Walsh's stomach. Janet Walsh was officially declared dead at 1:30 p.m. on Saturday, September 1. An autopsy was performed the same day, and the official cause of death was strangulation. There were no other signs of injury, such as stab wounds.

Pathologist Gary Marcus, who performed the autopsy, testified that he found ligature marks – skin bruises – on the neck and wrists, along with burst capillaries in the eyes that are typical of strangulation. He also found contusions – marks caused by blows – near the right ear and on a left portion of her face. He found no signs of struggle but did find trauma in the larynx that would be found in strangulation. The strangulation, Marcus testified, was caused by a ligature. The time of death, he specified, would have been between 5 and 7 a.m.

Under cross-examination, the doctor testified that he saw no dried semen on the body's wrists or hands; nor did he note any noticeable signs of dried semen on the nightgown. He saw no evidence or signs of rape.

***

The initial testimony of the trial's second day continued exploration of the investigative technicalities of the previous day from forensic pathologist Dr. James Smith and from state police Trooper Richard Matas. While confirming cause-of-death details for the prosecution, Smith's testimony enabled Ross in cross-examination to establish that Janet Walsh's clothing had been eyed visibly by the doctor and others and that nothing worth noting or requiring further analysis was found in that examination.

Matas, retired from the force by the time of the trial, confirmed for the court the evidence already established about the crime, including the neat state of Janet Walsh's apartment, a description of her body and its condition and positioning (face down on the bed), the collection and careful sealing of clothing, bedding, the kerchief used to strangle the victim, her nightgown, the bath robe cord used to bind her hands behind her – all accounted for and initialed by Matas – and the dusting for fingerprints, a process the defense would seize upon in cross-examination to buttress its argument on behalf of an investigation that, if not botched, was less than thorough.

But first, Ross in his cross-examination raised the issue of gloves, following up on Matas' testimony that he had worn gloves during the collection of evidence. This contradicted Gall's testimony from the day before, that no gloves were used in 1979.

Ross, setting the stage for the possibility of

tainted evidence, asked Matas if he had changed gloves during the collection of evidence, or if he'd worn the same pair throughout.

"I would not have changed gloves," Matas testified.

Moving on to the collection of fingerprints, Ross directed Matas' attention to a projected photo of Janet Walsh's lime green Monte Carlo and asked Matas to confirm that the fingerprint expert had been unable to match Janet Walsh's fingerprints to those lifted from the passenger side window of the car.

"That is correct," Matas testified.

"Now, wasn't it a possibility that whoever did this may have come home with Miss Walsh that night in her car?"

"Anything is possible, Mr. Ross."

Asked if any of the suspects at the time had been asked for their fingerprints for a possible attempt at comparison to those found on the passenger window, Matas said no.

"So, you had fingerprints from a vehicle that this young lady drove home at approximately four o'clock a.m.; you had latent prints lifted from that passenger side window that didn't match the victim, but there's no further steps taken to find out who those fingerprints belonged to, at least while you're involved; am I correct?"

"Correct," Matas responded. "I took no prints from anyone for further comparison."

Returning to the evidence collected in the apartment, Ross asked Matas if he had observed any stains or dried semen on Janet Walsh's nightgown.

No, responded Matas. Nor did the retired trooper see any stains or other markings on the robe tie or on the bandana around her neck. And he observed no dried semen on the victim's body.

Ross turned the court's attention to a tissue, seen in a photograph in front of the wastebasket, and asked Matas if he had collected it and the wastebasket, which was full of discarded tissues. He asked Matas if he thought it could be important to collect for analysis the tissues in the wastebasket and the one on the floor.

"At the time, obviously, I didn't deem it sufficiently evidentiary," Matas responded. "In hindsight, perhaps I made a mistake, and perhaps in light of what's transpiring here today, I should have collected that and that discarded tissue."

Finally, Ross returned to the possibility of tainted evidence by asking Matas if he had packaged the two bed sheets – the fitted, bottom sheet, and the top sheet, which covered the victim's body – in the same bag.

"Yes, I did."

As for all of the other items collected for evidence – the bed blanket, the victim's clothing and shoes, the pillow, sheets and a robe – nothing unexpected had been found in the crime lab analysis, testimony revealed.

Finally, asked by Ross if the crime scene had been reinvestigated or whether any of the primary suspects' clothing had been sought for analysis, Matas said no.

In an attempt to minimize the damage regarding possible tainted evidence or evidence not sought, Martocci, on redirect, pointed out that the initial investigation took place in 1979.

"Did you have in your mind at that time when you were collecting that evidence what DNA value could have been retrieved from the tissues or from the wastebasket?" he asked Matas.

"The incident takes place September 1 of '79. We are trying this case in 2013," Matas replied. "DNA was not even remotely thought of in 1979."

As for the unidentified fingerprints on the window of Janet Walsh's car, Matas testified that no follow-up was done because the information available to Matas indicated that Janet had left Perkins by herself.

Nonetheless, Ross had managed to put before the jury in this early testimony the possibility of an investigation that could have been more thorough and to raise questions regarding the possibility of one of the other original primary suspects being the culprit.

***

One of them, Janet Walsh's estranged husband, was next on the agenda, with prosecutor Smith questioning him in depth about his whereabouts the evening before and the early morning of her murder. Along the way, she elicited testimony indicating that Janet still harbored strong feelings for her husband, despite their estrangement – emotions that could play either way with the jurors, depending on their interpretation of love notes she had written in Scott's high school yearbooks the day before her death.

Scott Walsh was one of two of the original primary suspects put on the stand by the prosecution early in the trial, but such testimony might prove useful to both sides of the trial. Intended by the prosecution as a pre-emptive legal strike by eliciting testimony designed to demonstrate their innocence in Janet Walsh's death and thus to further implicate Hopkins, this tactic also opened the door for Ross to cast doubt on their stories and to divert attention from his client and to them.

Both witnesses – first, Scott Walsh, followed by Robert McGrail – offered Ross such opportunity.

After answering such preliminary questions as when he and Janet met (high school) and where they lived (in a home bought from his parents before purchasing the Ella Street house from a couple who had bought it from Hopkins) and whether he knew Hopkins (Walsh had met him once, he believed, in Margie Farinacci's driveway), Scott Walsh emphatically denied killing his wife, from whom he was then separated, but not divorced, because of difficulties due primarily to their financial problems.

"Mr. Walsh, did you kill your wife?" Smith asked at the conclusion of testimony from Walsh.

"I did not," said the 57-year-old Walsh, since remarried.

He did, however, see her the day before her murder as part of a relationship that he described as friendly despite the separation. At the time of her death, the couple were experiencing their second separation, after they had reconciled for about half a year beginning in January of 1979.

"I felt it was good," Scott Walsh testified of the couple's relationship. "We still always talked. She'd talk to me; I'd talk to her. We'd call each other all the time."

He did not have a key to Janet's apartment after she moved out of their Ella Street house, he said, but he had visited her there three or four times. But, he said, they'd never had sexual relations in her apartment. As for their sexual behavior while living together as man and wife, under questioning by Smith, Scott testified that his wife typically put a towel on top of the sheets so they would not have to be laundered afterwards. Also, he told Smith, his wife did own workman-style handkerchiefs or bandanas, which she wore when house-cleaning.

His wife had been hospitalized once during their separation, for a stomach ailment, he said, but he did not visit her in the hospital because "her parents would be there, and I think she just, she was upset at the situation, just upset that she was sick and upset that we were separating."

They had never filed for divorce, Scott testified, but as part of the legal separation he had agreed to give her $75 the first of each month, and "that check on September first might have been the first one."

The day before his wife's death, Scott told the court, he had gotten off work early because he and Janet were getting their house appraised for a possible sale. They planned to sell the house to help with their finances.

"We thought maybe if we sold our house, maybe we could make it once we were out of the debt, the burden of the house," he testified.

After the appraisal, Janet phoned him to see how it went, and then she told him she had signed his yearbooks while at the house earlier that day. So he went to the house to look at them.

In the 1971 Monaca High School yearbook – Janet's freshman year, his sophomore year – she wrote: "To Scotty. I'll always love you. Jan."

In the next year's book she wrote: "Scotty, we were meant to be. Always love you, Janet."

And the next year: "Scotty, love always, Janet."

After putting the yearbooks away, he went to a friend's house, and the two went out to dinner and then to the Beaver Falls-Blackhawk football game that evening. After the game, he said, they went to Stubby's restaurant for a drink and bite to eat. Afterwards, his friend got sick, "and it kind of escalated, kind of got pretty bad. So, he asked me if I'd take him to the Beaver Falls Hospital." This was about 11 or 11:30, Scott testified. He waited for his friend, then drove him to his Beaver Falls home before returning to his own Ella Street house at nearly 2 a.m.

After a few minutes, he got a call from a girl he'd been seeing.

"She was at a party on the other side of the hill with her sister, and she just said, 'what are you doing?' I said, 'I just got home.' She said, 'well, do you want me to stop over?' I said, 'yeah, if you want to.' So she came over."

The girl, a 17-year-old high school student, arrived a few minutes after 2 a.m., he testified, and she stayed about a half hour, during which time they engaged in oral sex. He fell asleep on his couch, he said, and the girl phoned about 50 minutes later to let him know she'd arrived home safely.

"I'm thinking it's around three-thirty, in that area, twenty-five to four, maybe," he told the court. He said he then went back to sleep and did not recall seeing Margie Farinacci arrive home next door.

The next morning, he testified, he went to Equibank in Beaver, then to the post office in

Monaca. He saw Peter Caltury on the sidewalk and waved as he drove by. After the post office, he went to Janet's house to drop off the support check. After she did not respond to his knocks on the door around noon, he dropped the check and the key ring from Reliable Refrigeration, which he had found while mowing his lawn, in the mail slot. Then Peter Caltury phoned him about 1 p.m., he said, with the news that Janet had been murdered.

"I don't know if he said she was murdered or she was strangled. My first reaction, I thought about my yearbooks, and I said, 'well, who did it? Did she do it?' I initially thought she might have taken her own life, after thinking of the yearbooks and everything she wrote to me. And he said, 'no.' "

Caltury asked him to come to the police station, where he saw both the father and the mother sitting in a chair.

"They were holding hands, and they were crying, and I knelt down in between them and um, they were a mess, and her mother looked at me, and she said, 'Scott, you didn't have anything to do with this, did you?' I said, 'Mrs. Caltury,' I said, 'I think you know the answer to that question.' She shook her head and said, 'I know you didn't.' "

After driving the parents back to Janet's Indiana Avenue house to pick up their car, he went to the parents' house and stayed about two hours until the police called and asked him to come in for questioning. He was there about 45 minutes, he testified, and had several encounters with the police after that.

"Every time they would call me and ask me to meet with them or do anything, I'd meet with them and do anything they wanted me to do."

He cooperated with the police, he said, "for thirty-two years."

Defense attorney Ross – knowing that when the trial moved to the subject of DNA testing, evidence would show that Scott Walsh's DNA also would be found on his wife's bed sheet – in his cross-examination seized on Walsh's narrative of the early morning hours of Janet's murder as well as exploring other issues that would throw doubt on the witness' veracity and credibility.

Ross began his questioning with a subject that had not come up during the prosecution's questioning – that the day of the initial police interview on September 1, 1979, Scott Walsh had told police he'd learned that Janet was involved in an affair with Scott Hopkins.

"I didn't know she was seeing anybody," Scott Walsh testified.

Ross referred the witness to a copy of his original statement to the police, in which Janet's friend Barbara Cinderich had told Scott Walsh that Hopkins and Janet "had a blowup on the phone a couple days before that." Scott conceded at this point that Hopkins and Janet perhaps were acquainted, and he testified that he could not remember other references in the statement about any knowledge he had of Janet knowing or seeing Hopkins. Also, Scott testified, after reading his original statement again, that he could not recall making the statement to the police that he had "tailed" Hopkins.

Moving on to the early morning hours of Janet Walsh's death, Ross projected a photo of the Walsh and Farinacci homes on Ella Street and established the fact that Scott was up early that morning after his encounter with his girlfriend and that he knew Janet was going out with Margie Farinacci the night before her death.

The Walsh home was on the right of the projection; the Farinacci home on the left.

As Margie pulled into her driveway after her night out, Ross asked, where would her headlights shine?

"Across my yard, then in front of her garage door."

"And there's no doubt you were up this morning, this particular night, around three-thirty or four o'clock, is there?"

"Three-thirty," Scott replied. "I don't know about four o'clock. I would say I'd be back asleep then."

Ross turned his attention to the banking conducted by Scott Walsh the next day, questioning why his cashed paycheck from St. Joe Zinc Company was stamped by National Bank of Beaver County when Walsh had testified that he cashed it at Equibank – one bank would have required a drive-by of Janet's apartment, the other (National Bank) would not.

Walsh insisted he'd cashed the check at Equibank.

Ross introduced two other elements intended to cast doubt onto Scott Walsh's testimony: that Scott had returned to Janet's apartment on September 15, 1979, with a police officer to retrieve two of Janet's bathrobes from the bedroom. ("I don't recall that," Scott testified), and that Scott and his wife had quarreled contentiously during a telephone conversation while she was in the hospital for the stomach ailment – "she was upset at the situation," Walsh testified.

***

Having thus planted some doubts about Scott Walsh, Ross also had what would be troubling questions for Robert McGrail, the stranger who had danced with Janet that Friday night and then accompanied her and Margie Farinacci to Perkins afterward – including the unexpected discovery of his checkbook on the street near Janet Walsh's apartment.

But first, Martocci would question McGrail extensively about his activities of that Friday night.

The scenario painted by Martocci was one of a single man on the prowl that evening, which ended with Janet Walsh rebuffing his advances at Perkins restaurant during the ensuing early morning hours.

Now working in the meat department of a convenience store/deli in Saugus, Massachusetts, the 64-year-old McGrail told the court that he had lived in Beaver County in the late 1970s, in a rental home, since destroyed in a fire, on Broadhead Road near the campus of Penn State/Beaver.

At the time, McGrail testified, he worked tending bar at a golf club in Ambridge and then for the Top of the Mall restaurant as a busboy/waiter. He also had worked as a maintenance man at Woolworth's, also located in the mall. That Friday, he got a call from a friend named Al Awad he'd met while working at the Top of the Mall asking if he wanted to go out that night. They decided to try a new club, the Getaway.

McGrail put on a sport coat, dress shirt and a pair of slacks, and Awad picked him up – McGrail was without a car, having totaled his in an accident shortly after arriving in Pennsylvania. McGrail also was low on funds and borrowed some cash from his friend.

After a few drinks – he consumed about five during the course of the evening, he testified – he approached Janet, whom he knew that evening by her first name, Catherine, and asked for a dance.

"And we danced, and I enjoyed – she was a very good dancer. She was a very friendly, personable person, you know."

They stayed on the floor after that first dance for several more, "and I got to talk to her a little bit at the table in between dancing."

"And how did you get along?"

"Very well. She was very friendly. I liked her. The first time you go out, you know how you try and meet someone, and so we danced, and the night progressed, and they closed, and prior to them closing, I think Al Awad had left early … He wasn't enjoying himself for some reason, to the best of my recollection. I don't know what happened, but he left. So I had not my ride home. So, I was going to see if I can get a ride with Catherine."

After the bar closed, McGrail said, he walked with Janet to Perkins, where he sat down with her, "and she was a little reluctant about, um, wanting to give me a ride. You know, she had just met me, and so she wasn't real sure about it, you know. So, we sat down, and so she said to me, she said, 'look.' She says, 'I'm going through a divorce, and my husband is a very jealous man, and if he saw me with – I never know when he may show up,' or something like that. So, she asked me if I would leave, more or less. She was pretty straightforward, that I could find another way home."

Asked how he felt about the rejection, he said he was, "a little surprised." But, he added, he was "agreeable. I mean, I wasn't angry or anything. I understand. I just met her. I never met her before."

So he left the table, he testified, and ran into a woman he knew from the Top of the Mall and from Woolworth's, and he joined her and forgot about Janet – Catherine – Walsh.

"I didn't pay attention to where Catherine went or whether she was still at the table."

He left the restaurant by himself, he testified, and walked up and then down a steep hill in the back of the parking lot that separated Perkins from the Penn State branch campus. It was a long walk home on the highway, he testified, and the campus "was a much shorter distance because my property abutted at the bottom of the hill."

He had to cross a creek and to step across an old wire fence, he said, "and you'd be on my property, and I could walk to my home."

When he arrived home he went straight to bed, he testified, sleeping heavily because he had been drinking, "and in the morning, must have been around ten, I'm just guessing, I can't remember exactly what time it was, the police were at the front door banging on the door, and they had the house with cruisers and all kinds of people there. Um, I didn't know what to make of it. You know, it startled me from sleeping. I just threw a pair of pants on. They asked me to come down;

they wanted to question me about something. They did not say what it was until I got to the police station."

The police questioned him for about an hour and then took him home. Then, a week or so later, he testified, the police contacted him again to ask about his checkbook, which had been turned in to them by a woman who found it near Janet Walsh's home.

"I recognized it right away," he said. "I didn't even know it was missing until they presented it in front of me. I didn't know it was missing." He said he had taken it with him the night he went to the Getaway in case he needed cash. He had put it in the pocket of his sport coat.

Ross, in his cross-examination, honed in on several of these points – the lost checkbook, McGrail's mood before and after being rejected by Janet, his long trek home over the hill, the arrival of the police at his home the next day.

Ross' questioning began with the drinking and dancing at the Getaway, in which he established that McGrail was "pretty intoxicated."

"I had a few drinks, yes."

Actually, Ross suggested, McGrail was so drunk that he slept until 4 p.m. the next day – not 10 a.m. as he had just testified – when the police knocked on his door.

"I had a hangover. Yeah, I slept late."

Having established McGrail's faulty memory, Ross went back to the early morning hours after the Getaway, when McGrail had joined Janet and Margie at Perkins, to again demonstrate McGrail's memory problems.

Referencing Janet's mention to McGrail of her husband's jealousy, Ross asked, "she just didn't tell you he was jealous, did she Mr. McGrail? She said he was violent, didn't she?"

"She said that he got angry, yes, that's correct."

"Did she tell you that her husband was violent?"

"She said he got upset. She was afraid of him."

Moving on to McGrail's testimony that he had given no more attention to Janet Walsh after leaving her table at Perkins, Ross again found contradictory testimony by referring to a videotaped interview that McGrail had conducted with Detective Gall in 2011.

"Isn't it a fact, sir, you kept looking over to see where she was?"

"I may have looked over there, yeah."

"Okay. So if you said that on that statement, would that be correct, the taped statement, that you kept looking over?"

"Well, like I say, it's thirty years ago. It's hard to remember exactly everything that I did at that particular time."

McGrail finally conceded that he had hoped for more than a ride home from Janet Walsh – that his aim was to be invited to her home.

"Well, I mean, I met her and you know, things happen when you're out like that, and sometimes you go back to your home or the other person's home," McGrail testified.

"And also, sir, were you hoping to date her?"

"Well," McGrail responded, "I would have liked to have dated her. Again, I liked her. She was a very nice person. I mean, she was a great dancer and was someone new."

Next came McGrail's drunken walk home after Janet had turned him down. It was rough terrain. Ross projected photos of the hill and the route that McGrail would have followed at about 4 a.m. that morning. Dressed in sport coat, slacks and dress shirt, he would have crossed a stream, a small fence and a marshy area to get home.

It was still dark, McGrail recalled, but he did not know the time of his arrival home.

Now what about that lost checkbook, Ross wanted to know.

McGrail again testified that he had no idea how he may have lost it, but he had worked up a sweat while dancing and had taken off his sport coat, in which he had stashed the checkbook, and hung it on the back of a chair. He didn't think of the checkbook again, he said.

"Did you ever go and report that checkbook lost or stolen?"

"I didn't know I'd lost it."

"Well, the police, according to the information I have, didn't even talk to you until about nine, ten days later. Are you saying during that time period you didn't know you lost your checkbook?"

"That's right. I did not know I lost that checkbook until it was presented to me at the police station."

***

At this point, the prosecution recalled Detective Gall to the stand, to lend context to all of the testimony – primarily by Scott Walsh and Robert McGrail – that had come since he first testified.

One issue revisited was Scott Walsh's return, with the police, to Janet Walsh's apartment several days after her murder to recover two robes – one of blue terrycloth, the other a maroon terrycloth robe. Neither was missing a belt or tie cord and thus would be of little further importance in this trial.

Martocci asked Gall if there was any evidence that Scott Walsh was a violent person.

"No."

When asked what came of the proceeds from the sale of the Walshes' house on Ella Street,

Gall said Scott had split them with the Caltury family.

At this point, Martocci moved to the subject that would come to dominate the latter days of the trial: DNA. Gall testified that Scott Walsh had volunteered a buccal swab, in which tissue is scraped from inside the mouth with a stick, for DNA analysis, and "the DNA found on the nightgown, the rope, the sheets was not Scott Walsh."

"Now," asked Martocci, "based on that and his interviews, then was he eventually eliminated as a person of interest?"

"In my mind, certainly."

Martocci moved the subject to McGrail, "the last person," Gall testified, "we know that, except for Margie Farinacci, who would have seen her alive or that we had known about at that time."

Was that the reason that police focused on McGrail, Martocci asked.

"That and the checkbook."

Gall then told the story of how police had come into possession of the checkbook. On September 7, after Wanda Jesky found the checkbook in the gutter of Ninth Street, which connects downtown Monaca to the Monaca-Rochester bridge, she turned it in at 10:30 that night to the Monaca Police Department. The gutter where the checkbook was found was about nine houses away from Janet Walsh's apartment.

Gall confirmed what McGrail had already stated – that McGrail said he had no recollection of losing the checkbook until police confronted him with it several days later.

Martocci then moved the questioning to the interview that Gall had flown to Massachusetts to conduct with McGrail in 2011. McGrail's testimony in this follow-up interview was consistent with his previous testimony the day of the discovery of Janet Walsh's body, Gall testified. The detective said that McGrail gave a buccal swab to police for DNA evidence and that the results of that analysis eliminated McGrail as a suspect.

Ross, though, was not done with the checkbook matter. Taking Gall back to the 2011 videotaped Massachusetts interview with Mc-Grail, attended by Gall and by a Massachusetts state trooper, when McGrail was still considered a suspect, he asked the detective if he had questioned McGrail about the checkbook.

"Extensively," Gall responded.

"And you didn't believe what he was telling you, did you?"

"Of course I did."

Here, Ross referred Gall and the court to the videotaped interview.

"You tell Mr. McGrail that day that there's too many holes in his story about the checkbook, right? Isn't that what you said?"

"Well," Gall responded, "we can say 'yes.' That's what I said. I think everybody here knows what we were doing there."

Ross: "You tell the man, 'you killed her like a dog, dropped your checkbook …' "

Gall: "Maybe you didn't …"

Moments later, following an objection from Martocci, Gall clarified:

"No, no. That was not me who said that. I was the man sitting in the chair. The trooper said that, playing the good guy-bad guy role, and I sat there and never said he killed her like a dog."

Ross: "But that day you told him there were too many holes in his story about the checkbook, didn't you?"

Gall: "Why do you think I would go all the way to Massachusetts?"

Ross: "But you just said you believed him."

Gall: "Absolutely. When that interview was over, and you're only playing a few seconds of it, that interview is over. That man never gave any indication that he was telling anything but the truth, the same way he did on the stand here today."

Ross moved the questioning to the DNA, suggesting that McGrail had not voluntarily offered the buccal swab sample.

"You actually had a search warrant in hand that day, right?"

"Yes I did," Gall responded.

"And you told him about it before he agreed to give it?"

"Yes." But, Gall added, "after we told him about the search warrant, he says, 'you don't need that. I will be glad to give it to you.' The only thing he wanted was an explanation on why we wanted it."

Ross at this point detoured back to Scott Walsh, producing an affidavit signed by State Trooper Rocco DeMaiolo, prepared in 2011 before Scott Walsh was ruled out as a suspect that indicated doubts about Scott Walsh's credibility.

Ross asked Gall to read from the document.

Gall complied, reading:

" 'Furthering belief that Mr. Walsh, in fact, is the individual responsible for the victim's death, is the fact that he was interviewed on at least five occasions by numerous experienced investigators who agreed that several of his responses to their questions indicated deception.' "

The defense attorney then offered a preview of his own DNA argument yet to come. He asked Gall about laboratory reports indicating that Scott Walsh's DNA was not at the scene of the murder. He asked Gall if he was familiar with a report that Ross had provided to the district attorney's office in November 2012 by a DNA forensics expert indicating that Scott Walsh's DNA was indeed found on Janet Walsh's bed sheets. He asked Gall if he had submitted that new data to the Pennsylvania State Police Laboratory for analysis.

He had not, Gall testified.

Ross then referred the detective to Scott Walsh's statement about following Scott Hopkins upon possibly learning that Hopkins and Janet had known each other or become involved. Ross asked Gall if it was correct that Scott Walsh had been represented in the 2011 search warrant as having tailed Hopkins.

Gall replied in the affirmative, adding that he did not believe Scott Walsh was tailing Hopkins before the murder, despite such a reference in a 2011 affidavit from DeMaiolo's 2011 search warrant. He added that he had not previously read DeMaiolo's document and therefore could not explain the discrepancy as to the conflicting statements about whether Scott Walsh had indicated that he was tailing Hopkins.

The judge intervened at this point to add some context: The original interviews conducted in 1979 were taped, using a tape recorder placed in the middle of the room, transcribed by people who were not professional stenographers. Thus, "there were numerous gaps, and there was some obvious mishearings of things."

***

In his testimony the next day, DiMaiolo would offer more perspective on Scott Walsh and what he knew about Hopkins, beginning with Ross asking the retired trooper if it was indeed his belief in 2011 that Walsh was being deceptive.

"Yes," the trooper replied.

Ross moved to Walsh's statement during his initial interview with police immediately following the discovery of the body on September 1, 1979.

Ross read aloud from DiMaiolo's affidavit:

" 'During the interview, Mr. Walsh,' and we are talking his interview on September 1st," said Ross, reading from the affidavit, " 'Mr. Walsh was asked if the victim had been dating anybody, and curiously his response was, "well, I asked her this morning or I asked her before, and she said, 'no.' " That's what you wrote in this?"

DeMaiolo: "Absolutely."

Ross: "And then you go on to state that Mr. Walsh describes tailing Mr. Hopkins and learning that he had been married but believed he was divorced now."

DeMaiolo agreed that he and Ross had reached the same conclusion regarding Scott Walsh knowing about and, apparently, tailing Hopkins.

Ross then moved on to the issue of Scott Walsh's paycheck and where he had cashed it on the day that Janet Walsh's body was found. Ross asked DeMaiolo to read aloud a specific portion of Trooper Frank Keenan's report concerning that paycheck. DeMaiolo complied.

DeMaiolo: " 'Check at St. Joe Zinc Company, Monaca, Pennsylvania, revealed that Walsh received his paycheck on 31 August, '79. A photostat of the check showed that same was cashed on 4 September, '79 at the Beaver Trust Bank in Beaver, Pennsylvania. Subject will be re-interviewed concerning this discrepancy. A copy of the check is attached to the report.' "

Ross: "Nowhere does it reflect Beaver Trust or Equibank, does it?"

DeMaiolo: "No."

Ross: "Did anybody ever follow up to your understanding, and please feel free to look at your reports, with Scott Walsh about this?"

DeMaiolo: "No."

At this point, the trial would shift to the scientific, DNA portion of the evidence – to the breakthrough technological findings that had brought about the day of revelation leading to DeMaiolo's knees buckling when he learned that semen was found on the evidence kept in storage all these years.

DeMaiolo, who took over the case in 1997 and was the last in the line of troopers put in charge of the Walsh murder investigation, offered the court his opinion that this cold case had suddenly warmed up considerably thanks to that finding.

"Because of the position of the body," he testified near the end of the trial's third day, "that the fact that semen was found on the back of the nightgown, on the ropes that actually were binding her hands, and the bed sheet but more importantly those two items, that this was going to be the killer's DNA."

Following that dramatic statement, Ross traced the forensic history of the case: from the belief beginning in the 1980s and onward that "this was actually a case that was reported as not involving a sexual assault," Ross observed, citing the inability of crime lab personnel as recently as 2005 to find "observable trace evidence" on the clothing and other items stored by the state police.

Ross referred DeMaiolo to the witness' May 6, 2005 report in which he summarized a discussion with Chris Arrotti, a supervisor at the state lab, in which he concluded that the blue bandana used to strangle Janet Walsh "would contain the best trace evidence for purposes of this case" but which, in fact, revealed no DNA.

Five years later, Ross continued, records from a meeting involving DeMaiolo and lab personnel indicated that the original seals on the envelopes containing the evidence had become degraded; DeMaiolo agreed. Finally, Ross used the occasion of redirect questioning of DeMaiolo to draw the court's attention to a finding, by a defense DNA forensics expert, of Scott Walsh's DNA and of "an unidentified third person" among the evidence submitted to the lab.

But the key DNA-related evidence of the day came after DeMaiolo was brought back to the stand – after testimony by borough officials about collecting Hopkins' discarded drinking cup for use as a DNA sample, which was turned over to DeMaiolo for testing at the state lab – followed by Detective Gall.

***

Both men testified that the DNA obtained from Hopkins' drinking cup had matched the DNA found on items from the evidence collected on the day of discovery of Janet Walsh's body – including the cord used to bind her hands, and her nightgown.

Gall testified that the DNA obtained voluntarily from the other four suspects – Scott

Walsh, Robert McGrail, Ron Ciccozzi and Carlo – had eliminated them and focused attention of the investigation on Hopkins. Gall testified that Hopkins' DNA also was found on the flat sheet – the one that partially covered Janet Walsh's body.

Prosecuting attorney Martocci then asked Gall to testify about the length of time it would take to drive from the model home where Hopkins was living then, during his separation from his wife, to Janet Walsh's apartment.

Gall said it took about ten minutes during a noon test drive of the 6.3-mile distance on a weekday, "where the traffic was heaviest." It would not have been as heavy during the early morning hours, he said.

Gall then summarized for the jury facts the reader already knows about this case: that Hopkins, after first denying that he knew Janet Walsh except only to see her, then admitted to engaging in a secret sexual affair with Janet; that he had visited her at her apartment late at night or early in the morning during the affair; that Hopkins was alibied the day of the murder by friends, including a girlfriend he was seeing while separated from his wife, who were at his model home overnight to help prepare for a Labor Day weekend pig roast that Saturday; that Hopkins or his corporation owned a Porsche, a Rabbit, a Jeep Cherokee and three pickup trucks. Also, Hopkins had told police that he and a friend who managed the office at his construction company, Larry Musgrave, had gone out for drinks a couple of times with Margie Farinacci and Janet Walsh after construction meetings at the Holiday Inn on Wednesday nights. Hopkins, Gall said, told the investigating officers that the last conversation he'd had with Janet was when he'd called her about a week before her death at 11 p.m. or midnight – the typical time of their conversations and his visits to her – "to see what she was doing, and she was sleeping, 'and I said, "okay. Fine." I said, "I'll talk to you later,' " and that was, and that's as far as we've gone."

Hopkins had told officers that he learned of Janet Walsh's death when Margie Farinacci's husband, Joey, called on Saturday, September 1, to tell him they couldn't come to the party because Margie was not feeling well and, " 'well …

you know, Janet was murdered last night.' "

***

In his effort to clear Hopkins of that murder, Ross had by this point of the trial successfully sowed the seeds of doubt and possibly mistrust of some of the testimony – based on evidence of a reportedly jealous, angry and violent estranged husband who had opportunity after an early morning session of oral sex with a teenager to slip out of his house as soon as he knew his wife's companion of that fateful evening and early morning had arrived home; of a drunken and spurned single man on the make who couldn't explain how his checkbook ended up a few houses from the murdered woman's house; of differing or altered remembrances of events of more than three decades prior; of evidence not gathered or mishandled and thus compromised; of questions and avenues not pursued by police – in an investigation with some integrity issues.

One of those avenues, based on the advent of DNA analysis and evidence, would become the primary focus of the remainder of this trial.

7

We turn now to the other end of the telephone line of that phone call to Trooper DeMaiolo that buckled his knees. It came from forensic scientist Ashlee Mangan, who was calling DeMaiolo to let him know that sperm had been found on the bedding, tie rope and nightgown of the articles saved from the Walsh murder.

The task of the prosecution team at this stage of the trial became to convince the jury, as DeMaiolo had been convinced, that the DNA analysis was the key to assigning guilt in this murder. But the science leading to that finding is a bit complicated. It involves light technology, water extraction, counting sperm cells and DNA analysis. The prosecution built its case in carefully planned steps by first establishing the basics of the science involved, followed by applying the science to the evidence in this particular case.

Then would come testimony from a renowned criminal forensics expert to explain just how the perpetrator went about committing the crime, finishing with connecting the whole bundle of evidence to Hopkins.

As Martocci and Smith built the blocks of their case, Ross in his cross-examination tried to topple them with questions and evidence aimed at discounting the infallibility of the science and portraying the scientists, lab technicians and police agents as working in cahoots with police and prosecutors by using selective sampling and testing to implicate Hopkins while ignoring the possible culpability of the other primary suspects. This latter scenario included the findings of Scott Walsh's DNA on a sheet and of DNA from an unknown person on a robe.

***

The first block in the construction of the prosecution's scientific legal edifice was the testimony of Chris Arrotti, forensic laboratory manager at the Pennsylvania State Police Crime Laboratory's Greensburg lab, where she began in 1992 as a serologist and trace analyst. This latter responsibility included analyzing materials ranging from hairs and fibers to vehicle lamps, glue, explosive residues and paint. The purpose of this testimony was to school the jurors in DNA technology – primarily, in this case, the use of a relatively new tool known as alternate light source. Using this technology, analysts wear goggles to protect their eyes while studying the evidence employing a light that uses an altered wave length that, according to Arrotti, helps identify foreign material, such as stains in fibers "due to their ability to fluoresce. Fibers, especially the pinks, oranges, and red, will fluoresce," she testified. "Makeup, there's a long list of things that will fluoresce.

"But what it does now is it really helps us to look at things we may not have considered in the past, and they will do additional testing," she explained to the court.

"So that's one of the key approaches with a cold case is to use the alternate light source on the evidence."

Using the alternate light source, said Arrotti, analysts look not only for fluorescence, but also for "a different appearance. Sometimes it's a different color. Sometimes they would fluoresce, but you would see a difference in the fabric, and it would actually permit you to see the edges of a potential stain." This method would enable detection of saliva and "potential seminal stains … sometimes a urine stain, if you had to test for that as well."

The lab acquired its first alternate light source around 1994, so it was not available as a forensic tool in 1979, when the articles from the Walsh case were analyzed by Ralph Plankenhorn, a generalist who then handled not only serology but also trace evidence, blood alcohol, and drug detection, Arrotti explained under cross-examination by Ross.

"He was not limited to one discipline" in his analysis of the nine items of evidence, including a rape kit, in which he searched for blood, semen and hair (pubic and other types, including from another individual), she said. Back in 1979, the process was pretty much a visual examination, running hands across materials to detect stiffness, an indicator of a semen stain, known as a textile exam. And Plankenhorn "couldn't find any signs of a stain or trace evidence," Ross noted.

Under re-direct examination by Martocci, Arrotti went into greater detail of the findings coaxed from fibers with the use of alternate light source.

"You would see a variety of colors. Sometimes the stains you would not be able to see. Sometimes they would be ever so slightly a pale yellow. You would sometimes even see tan or brown. The more tan or brown that you saw, the more blood vessels were broke during ejaculation, and that's why you had more color.

"Sometimes it would even be pink," she continued, "because there would be so much blood with the semen, but typically they were colorless to a tan. There were items where sometimes I would look at them and I would circle stains that I saw visually and then I would turn on the alternate light source and I would look and I would see additional stains.

"Some of the fluorescent stains were positive for semen, some were negative. Some of the visual stains were positive. Some were negative."

In 2005, Arrotti, in conjunction with Christine Tomsey, who was the director of the DNA lab, asked Trooper DeMaiolo to submit the bandana or a piece of it from around Walsh's neck because, said Arrotti, it was determined that the light blue bandana ligature "presented the best possibility for trace DNA from the actor." DNA analysts, she said, would need to be questioned about what they were looking for in 2005 – an issue that the attorneys would leave for future testimony.

***

The prosecution's next DNA case-building block came from forensic scientist Ashlee Mangan of the serology section of the Pennsylvania State Police Bureau of Forensic Services at the Greensburg facility.

"We do body fluid identification," Mangan testified under questioning by Smith. "We analyze items of evidence that are submitted to the lab by law enforcement for bodily fluids. We identify blood and semen and detect saliva, urine and fecal material.

"I also identify hair as being human or animal, and we assist in blood stain pattern analysis at crime scenes or from photographs and on items of evidence as well."

Her goal, with the assistance of alternate light source, was to "either identify or detect bodily fluids that may be on the items of evidence," she testified. "I would then prepare samples for subsequent analysis by our DNA division … Once I either identify or detect a stain I would cut the sample out, place it in a clean envelope, and seal it, and it goes into a heat-sealed plastic container."

She continued: "Depending on what I am able to send for DNA analysis, sometimes we are limited to what we can send, and sometimes I retain samples in the laboratory. Sometimes they do get returned to the law enforcement department, and sometimes they go to the DNA lab."

She became involved in the Walsh case in November of 2010, she testified, when the evidence was brought to her – along with the background information, crime scene photos, previous lab reports and previous autopsy reports. "I got a lot of information about the case." This helped her determine what she could test for, "what stains would be helpful for the case," she said.

She analyzed the bandana under the alternate light source and got fluorescence around the knotted area. So she cut the knot, which was in the center, placed it in a clean envelope and prepared it for DNA analysis. She also looked at the bed sheets, where fluorescence also indicated staining, and she used a process that included applying water to the fibers to extract evidence.

"When I take the cutting, I let it extract in water for a period of time," she testified. "Because of the age of this, I let them extract overnight … I try to extract the material for any debris cells that may be present on the cutting."

She makes a microscope slide, puts the extract on it and dries it in an oven. She then uses a biological stain, which colors the nucleus of the cells red and stains the other cellular material green. The next part of the process is to count the number of sperm cells present.

"If I find one sperm head, two sperm heads, maybe up to five on that entire slide, I would give that a rating of one-plus. There is a scale that goes to four-plus, which would be the most."

On the fitted (bottom) bed sheet, she graded two of the areas as one-plus, she testified. The blue bath robe, from which the binding cord came, also yielded a one-plus; she found one sperm head on the front right side near the belt loop. She found sperm at the four-plus level in two sections of the blue top sheet, and the same level on the cord used to bind the victim's hands: The "entire rope had a glow to it and … certain areas had a, more of a glow to it" under the alternate light source, she said. She also got a four-plus reading on the nightgown top, where sperm was found on the middle back portion of the garment.

Mangan testified that she also received two drinking cups that had been used by Gregory Scott Hopkins, which she swabbed and sent to the DNA lab for analysis.

In his cross-examination, Ross had a question about a notation he had seen indicating that the person who brought the evidence items to Mangan suggested that "they were not properly sealed?"

"That is here, yes," she responded, which could mean something so simple as no evidence tape, or there may not have been a signature, date, or time, "but I don't know what she (the person delivering the evidence to Mangan) saw."

Ross also wondered if the clothing on the ironing board had been brought in for testing – it had not. And he noted that Plankenhorn found no observable trace evidence on that clothing in 1979. Mangan testified that in 2010 she also tested the rape kit; she found no sperm in the vaginal swab or in the oral swab.

Ross then asked a long series of questions about the fact that numerous items of evidence fluoresced under the alternate light source, but because no sperm was identified on them, no further testing, including water extraction for microscope analysis, was done.

"So the only thing you looked for in your

examination was sperm?" he asked.

Why?

"She was naked from the waist down, I thought maybe a sex act had occurred, so I was looking for semen," responded Mangan, who said it was solely her decision to look for sperm, though she had consulted with investigators.

Sixteen other areas fluoresced on the sheet. But they were not tested further.

Other fabric evidence brought similar decisions – not to test for the presence of any other DNA which, Ross suggested, could have been deposited by any of the other suspects, unless it was seminal.

"Can we further agree here that you found sperm in two areas, correct?" Ross asked of the flat bed sheet.

"Yes."

Ross: "Those areas could contain body fluids, saliva, grease from the hands, epithelial cells, could they not?"

Mangan: "They could have."

Ross: "But they were never tested, right?"

Mangan: "Not further. Once I found the

stain, I sent the best stain for DNA."

Ross: "The sperm stains?"

Mangan: "Yes."

Ross: "No one ever went back and checked these?"

Mangan: "I didn't, no."

In her initial analysis, Mangan said, she spoke with Jeff Fumea (at the time a supervisor in the DNA division) and Angela Biondi (at the time a forensic scientist in the DNA division). They told her what to send over and what not to send, Mangan testified. At first, they did not want to test the sheet.

Ross: "And they say ... they did not want to take the seminal stains from the sheets due to the information that she had sex with multiple individuals since her separation from her husband; correct?"

Mangan: "Yes."

But once the rape kit was negative for DNA, the district attorney decided to have the sheets sent over "because unless there is sperm on the fitted sheet, 'we can't allude to a jury that there was sexual activity,' " said Ross, reading from an email sent by DeMaiolo.

Ross next wondered if Mangan had been concerned that the sheets were placed in the same package and whether the DNA findings could help determine when the sperm was deposited on the sheets, tie cord and nightgown.

"Usually we like to have separate packaging for items," she testified, "but the sheets lay on top of one another during sleeping, so it wasn't a very big concern."

Ross: "But they were now contaminated, right, because two had been packaged together for 31 years?"

Mangan: "Yeah, they, it's nice to have them separated, so they do not touch or cross transfer, but they were from the same, they were both the victim's and they were on the bed together, so ..."

So, Ross asked, if the stains lasted for 31 years, they could then easily have lasted four, six or eight weeks before September of 1979 until the date of the murder?

Mangan: "Yes, my testing doesn't tell time of deposit."

Ross: "Did you ever consider in going

down this road of only looking for sperm that some of the people involved may have had prior sexual relations with Miss Walsh before September first of 1979?"

Mangan: "Did I try to? Is that what you're asking?"

Ross: "Did you consider that?"

Mangan: "I don't contact people."

Finally, Ross read from an email that Detective Gall had sent to Mangan on August 17, 2012, in which Gall speculated that Ross' theory of the crime was that the sperm deposited on the blue robe was " 'from a prior incident of sexual contact. If that is true, then the robe should have sperm from Hopkins on it. If there are no stains, the rope would probably have been removed from the robe when the sperm was deposited. If there is a white mark, it would show he used the robe to clean himself off. This needs to be examined as soon as possible.' That's what it says, doesn't it?"

"Yes," responded Mangan.

Ross: "So, in other words, if there is no sperm DNA on the robe, Mr. Hopkins is guilty, and if there is sperm on it, he is guilty, because he took the robe off to wipe himself. That is what it says; right?"

Mangan: "I think that's what he's saying."

A subsequent email from Mangan to a state police officer, said Ross, reading from the statement, said that Mangan did not believe the strangling cord came from that particular robe, that the " 'material of the rope should be the same as the robe. I told him I extracted 46 areas of the robe and six areas from the tissue I found in the back of the robe. I told them of my results, and I would be sending them five samples'; correct?"

Mangan: "Yes."

Ross: "So once you get the robe at the laboratory you're telling the police that that robe tie doesn't even match the robe, am I right?"

Mangan: "It's just an observation, yes."

Pointing to the robe in the courtroom, Ross asked Mangan if it was likely that whoever was in Janet Walsh's apartment the day of her murder handled the robe.

"It's possible," she replied.

Ross: "Why were you only testing for sperm?"

Mangan: "That is what I was looking for. The sperm cells, they last longer. They have better DNA than, if you want me to test for skin cells, I don't test for skin cells."

She did, she testified, find 45 other areas that fluoresced but did not have sperm but could have carried body fluids, saliva or epithelial cells.

The robe, Ross said, was within feet of where the murder occurred, "seven months after my client was charged, and all we're looking for is sperm, right?"

Mangan: "Yes."

Ross: "Were you aware of the fact that the police gave two robes back to the husband fourteen days after the incident?"

Mangan: "I don't recall."

In redirect by Smith, Mangan testified that she believed the murder still could have been connected to sexual activity despite the lack of sperm in the victim's vagina or mouth.

"Sometimes ejaculation does not occur inside the body," Mangan testified. "Sometimes a condom is used. It could be ejaculated somewhere else other than inside the body."

"Is it possible," Smith asked, "that somebody ejaculated on top of her?"

Mangan: "Yes."

As for the possibility of transfer of sperm cells from one sheet to the other after the sheets were packaged together, Mangan testified that a four-plus rating would not have been typical when the items that were packaged were dry. The four-plus rating, Mangan said, was significant because "it's a lot of semen there," and such a high rating would not be consistent with the bedding being washed.

***

The next task for Martocci and Smith was to move the gathering of the evidence from the serology testing to analysis of the DNA. This responsibility fell to Angelina Biondi, forensic DNA science supervisor at the state police lab's Forensic DNA Division.

Smith's first step at this stage was to fill in the gap between the lab's first assessment of the DNA in 2005 and the final scientific examinations and analysis a half-decade later that led to Hopkins.

Biondi told Smith that the first DNA sample was from the bandana that was used to strangle Janet Walsh, which was the only evidence submitted at that time. Biondi said no profile could be obtained from that sample. So, the case was put on hold until April of 2011, when Biondi analyzed seminal stains, which had come from the serology lab, from the nightgown and from the white cord used to bind the victim's hands.

The process that Biondi described to obtain the DNA from the sperm was a sort of chemical cleansing to remove the non-sperm DNA as much as possible. When the process was completed, Biondi testified, she was able to identify a previously unidentified profile from the sperm fraction obtained from the nightgown and also from the white cord, which yielded a partial profile. The profiles from these two samples matched and were found to be "consistent with a male," Biondi testified. And, she testified, the sample from the cord and from the nightgown would be from "the same unknown," or the same man.

The DNA profile was submitted to CODIS, but this search yielded no hits.

At this point, anticipating the defense line of questioning, Smith opened the door to potential degradation of the samples due to their age of more than 30 years. Specifically, she asked Biondi, "can your DNA degrade to the point where it looks like somebody else's DNA?"

Conceding that the samples were degraded – affected by exposure to natural elements that include sunlight and humidity – Biondi said the degradation might "reduce the amount of results that I get from a profile, but it would not change my profile."

Smith: "So the answer is it would not degrade into somebody else's DNA?"

Biondi: "Correct."

Biondi next testified that she received a buccal swab from Scott Walsh's mouth cheek, and there was no match to the samples found on the cord or nightgown.

With the removal of Scott Walsh as a suspect in the eyes of the jury, Smith turned the questioning over to Ross. The defense attorney began his task of raising doubts regarding both the validity and limits of the evidence and the investigative process involved in the science. He did this by establishing the credibility and methodology of his own expert witness, Dr. Mark Perlin, who would be called to testify when the trial moved to the defense portion.

He asked Biondi who had provided the instruction in her 2011 annual training session for the lab. "Dr. Mark Perlin," she replied.

Ross: "And he provided training for your entire laboratory?"

Biondi: "Yes."

In that training, Biondi and her colleagues learned about a computer method of analysis that Ross identified as TrueAllele, which differs from other state police methods and studies because of the heavy reliance on computer analysis and interpretation of all information.

Having completed what a novelist might call foreshadowing of events to come, but what lawyers call simply laying the legal groundwork for future arguments, Ross turned to Biondi's analysis of the samples, which she had received in

2010 but had not begun to analyze until the next April, of 2011.

He wondered why serologist Mangan and Biondi's supervisor, Fumea, did not originally want an analysis done of the bed sheets "that would have sperm on them to go along with the robe tie and the nightgown?"

"What we like to get into the laboratory first," Biondi answered, "is what would be the most probative items in that there would be little to no question as to whether they're important for investigative information."

At that point, she and Fumea were making the determination of what was probative – evidence of proof – based on the recommendation from serologist Mangan.

Biondi testified that the DNA testing could not determine when and how the DNA was deposited, nor whether the DNA was deposited on the cord at the same time as on the nightgown.

Returning now to his looming expert witness, Perlin and his yet-to-come testimony, Ross gave the court a preview and told Biondi that Perlin had found DNA from Scott Walsh on one of the sheets. He asked if she had ever been asked to compare samples from the sheet with the Walsh profile.

"I did not receive any more evidence in this case," she testified. "This case was taken over by another forensic scientist."

Also, Ross foreshadowed, evidence from Perlin would indicate the presence of DNA from an unknown, third person on the blue robe. He asked if she had been asked to submit anything from the blue bathrobe to CODIS.

"No."

On redirect, Smith, going back to the 2005 analysis of the strangulation bandana, asked if what the analysts were looking for at the time was "touch DNA," which comes from skin cells.

Such sampling, Biondi said, would provide less DNA than would a seminal stain, "and with our testing we can't see it unless we have it tagged fluorescently."

At this point, timing intervened to interfere with the step-building process. This was a Friday, and forensic scientist Dr. Cyril Wecht would not be available for testimony on Monday.

So the judge and lawyers, in consultation out of jury earshot, decided to finish the day's testimony with Wecht and to then come back to DNA forensic analyst Laura Brown – tasked with tying Hopkins' DNA to the samples obtained from the evidence – on Monday.

Jurors would soon learn why the defense had strenuously objected to forensic pathologist, doctor and lawyer Wecht as an expert witness and why the prosecution had taken the judge's ruling against Wecht's participation in the trial to a higher court.

***

Working from medical reports and photographs, among other evidence, the former longtime Allegheny County coroner and chief forensic pathologist began his testimony by dismissing any notion that bruises found on Janet Walsh's face were the result of facial impact against any part of the bed but were the "kinds of superficial contusions ... (that) can be produced by pressure, fingers, pressing down on an area, especially women will bruise usually more readily, so you can produce that kind of mild superficial contusion by applying strong pressure to those areas."

So, according to Wecht, the victim apparently was not beaten by her killer.

Other bodily injuries, internal and external, Wecht testified, are "all part of a picture of strangulation, direct pressure applied to tiny capillaries, the very tiniest blood vessels in the body that connect arteries and veins or small arteries, arterials, or small veins, veinals, and if you apply pressure to those, they can burst and a little bit of blood can leak out."

Janet Walsh may have suffered a torturous strangulation death, depending on the amount of force applied in the process, Wecht revealed in detailed testimony that enabled the jury to vividly understand what she experienced in her final moments.

Strangulation is not instantaneous, he explained. "First of all, any of us in good health and so on, we've got enough oxygen in our brain to keep us alive for four to six minutes if we were deprived of all oxygen. We would begin to lose consciousness. Then we would go on to die, but in a normal environment we could stay alive for four to six minutes, and strangulation depends on how forceful is the application, how intense, and how continuous.

"So, you know, I can't tell you, but let's just say if it is applied forcefully and the pressure remains, then you are going to lose consciousness probably anywhere from twenty, forty seconds, something like that, if it's complete. It it's less than complete, you can remain conscious longer.

"Then you begin to lose consciousness slowly, an ingravescent or downward course. It doesn't just turn off in one second, and then you would remain alive, as I've said, for another four minutes or so. But if the pressure continues and no blood gets up to the brain with oxygen, you will die."

Prosecuting attorney Martocci then moved to the two central issues raised by Wecht in his report on the case, one of which was how the semen was likely deposited on the three areas that the seminal fluid matched to Hopkins was found:

Justice Delayed

the flat (cover) sheet, the nightgown, and the cord used to bind the victim's hands.

Martocci led into the testimony by pointing out that the defense had suggested the occurrence of sexual activity between Hopkins and Janet Walsh three or four weeks before her death: "How would that or how did you consider that information in relation to the location of where you gleaned from those reports that the DNA was?"

Wecht responded that "topographical distribution" was behind the deposit of the seminal fluid on the three locations. The position of the body was face down, he said; "that was the result of an ejaculation, a male ejaculation that occurred as the victim was lying down and that some of the ejaculate got … in those locations."

Wecht said he found it difficult to believe that the deposits being analyzed were the result of activity from three to four weeks prior to the murder.

"For me, from an investigative analytical standpoint, to conceive that somehow four weeks have gone by and she has not thoroughly washed a sheet that she sleeps under, that she has not washed a belt of a bathrobe that she uses, that she's still wearing a nightgown that she sleeps in, I just find that extremely unlikely and it is on all of those findings that I express the opinion that I did."

Next came a key item of testimony about the evidence, in which Wecht described what indeed would have been not only a violent act but a sexual one – evidence that was not detected in the rape kit, for which there was no finding of sperm in any of Janet Walsh's cavities.

"In order for the ejaculate to be found as it was on the parts of the materials posteriorly, then the ejaculation would have had to have occurred from the individual on top of her," Wecht explained, "not while she obviously could not have been under here, and nothing to indicate that it had occurred and then her body was turned over."

Martocci asked if Wecht gave weight to finding that the lack of DNA evidence in the fingernail scrapings from Janet Walsh was a significant factor.

"No," Wecht testified. While fingernail clippings are routinely submitted and analyzed for DNA, forceful scratching must have occurred. That was an unlikely scenario based on the position of the body, the fact that the hands were tied and that, in Wecht's belief, the murderer was on top of the victim's back.

Next, anticipating the testimony to come from the defense attorney's expert witness, Perlin, Martocci steered Wecht in a direction intended to deflect the expected defense arguments that would include migration or transportation of the sperm from other areas.

Martocci wanted to know Wecht's opinion regarding the effect on the DNA samples of possible laundering of the materials or of cross-contamination.

Wecht said he was aware of the possibility of seminal fluid transference during the process of washing. But he found that to be unlikely in this case; it would have been "remarkably fortuitous that there would have been such contamination resulting in the deposition then of seminal material in those three places that you have contamination from the washing that Miss Walsh would have undertaken presumably by herself, out come the garments and so on, and lo and behold there are the seminal stains right there where she was found bound on that bathroom rope, on the nightgown, and on the sheet that overlies it in that area.

"I just, just can't accept that kind of explanation" that the sort of cross-contamination conjectured would occur in only those three areas, he concluded.

Martocci asked Wecht to elaborate on the first sentence of the final paragraph of his report, in which he concluded that no evidence supported the possibility of third-party involvement in the murder. Wecht responded with a lengthy elaboration, combining current DNA evidence implicating only one individual with historical criminology, to discount any other scenario regarding this death but his own.

"If these seminal stains had indeed been deposited approximately four weeks before, then you have still a dead body of Miss Walsh. You have her there bound in this exposed position and so on, where is the evidence of the person who would have bound her and done with her whatever it was that he did?

"There is a principle we have in forensic science, Locard, capital L, o-c-a-r-d, named after a famous French criminalist of the early part of the twentieth century that when there is contact between two people, there will be a transfer of evidence, and that's amazing because that was sixty years before DNA and years before homicide detectives and forensic scientists began to think about forensic evidence of a minute nature and so on.

"So you have a situation that required some involvement by somebody, the tying of the wrists, the tying of the handkerchief around the neck, the positioning of the body, and so on.

"For all of that to have been consummated, to have been executed without evidence of DNA, especially with the evidence of some kind of sexual activity, whether aborted or not, but I'm not going to get into that, but the absence is significant, too, and goes along with the positive findings."

In his cross-examination, Ross returned to a previous line of questioning in which he wondered why police officers, in their original investigation of 1979, could not find evidence on the robe tie or the nightgown of semen ejaculation just five to six hours after the murder.

Wecht said he could not explain that.

Ross asked if the stains could have been old stains.

"They were found then in 2010, 2011, so if they were old stains, they would just have become older, but they were found," Wecht responded. "They were not found in 1979. They weren't looked for. They weren't recognized. Maybe it wasn't the most thorough investigation in the world, I don't know."

And there was no ultraviolet light or fluorescent light technology then, Wecht testified.

Ross then explored Wecht's relationship with Perlin, whom Wecht had asked to write a chapter for the five-volume "Forensic Sciences" that was published in 2012 and whom Wecht had asked to serve on the board of the Wecht Institute of Forensic Science and Law at Pittsburgh's

Duquesne University.

Wecht testified that he had high regard for Perlin and his work in the field of DNA.

So, Ross asked, what about Perlin's finding, in his report, of other people's DNA "on some of the items in question?"

Conceding that the DNA of an unknown person had been found along with DNA matching that of Scott Walsh on a sheet, Wecht said these findings did not alter his assessment.

"Mr. Walsh was her husband and had obviously been in close proximity over an extended period of time," Wecht testified, adding that he factored this information into his analysis.

In response to Ross' questioning about the lack of spermal DNA in Janet Walsh's body cavities, Wecht suggested sexual activity that did not involve penetration.

"I'm not going to get off into a discussion, but there are all kinds of sexual games that are played and different ways that people engage in sexual activity, aberrational or for some people not considered an aberration, just part of the sex game," he said.

Ross: "Doctor, isn't it possible that this was not a sex crime at all just an outrageous murder, someone trying to strangle her, and the DNA has absolutely nothing to do with this?"

Wecht: "No, sir. I don't believe so because of the findings, and again I want to say that I have received, as you know, all of the reports and so on, and I'm aware there was no evidence of any kind of a break-in, robbery, burglary, ransacking or so on, no evidence of a struggle, no evidence of her having been beaten and so on.

"So the idea that somebody came in, I don't know what they would have come for then, what they would have done, just go ahead and kill her in that position, I'm sorry, I just can't envision that as I think about my cases over half a century."

At this point, Wecht conceded information that supported Ross' earlier contention of an investigation not pursued extensively enough. He agreed with Ross that seeking only sperm under the alternate light source was too limiting.

"I do think that there could have been more studies, yes," he testified.

And, Ross asked, was it a mistake to disregard 45 places fluorescing on the bathrobe because no sperm was there?

Wecht: "Well, not for me to say whether a mistake. I certainly would agree that those are things that could have been tested for, yes."

Wecht gave a similar response when asked about the failure to test the non-sperm fluoresced areas on the tie cord.

"These are things that could have been tested for depending on the time, the circumstances, the techniques, the money available for testing, the degree of educational background," Wecht testified. "There's a lot of things that would have been factors."

Wecht gave the same answer regarding the failure to test the non-spermal findings on the sheets. Similarly, he agreed that other items found at the crime scene "might have been considered."

Wecht offered a more forceful agreement regarding mistakes made when he testified that anal swabs of Janet Walsh should have been taken.

"I would do anal swabs certainly in every

case like this," he testified. "That I do believe was a mistake."

Ross returned to Wecht's testimony about time involved in strangulation death, but he now wanted to explore how the body reacts to this sort of stress – including a more rapid heartbeat and the possibility that the victim might sweat. The attorney asked about the possibility of an old seminal stain becoming wet from such perspiration and transferring from the nightgown to the tie cord, or if the urine that the victim expelled during strangulation could have transferred from the back of the nightgown when she was rolled onto her back by investigators the following day.

Wecht discounted these possibilities. "I just can't envision it."

Finally, in redirect, Martocci used Wecht's testimony – his reading of Perlin's looming report – to match Hopkins' DNA to that found on the samples discussed above: tie cord, nightgown and the flat cover sheet.

"Doctor, who does Dr. Perlin attribute those three areas where we had that high density rating to?" Martocci asked, referring to the high-sperm finding on the three areas.

"Mr. Hopkins," Wecht responded.

Martocci: "And his probabilities in that area of the nightgown compared to anyone else that he compared to that nightgown, it's only who?"

Wecht: "Mr. Hopkins."

Ditto for the tie cord.

The match of Hopkins' DNA to that found on the tie cord, the nightgown and the sheet was the final building block in the prosecution's construction of its scientific case. All that remained for the following Monday was for the prosecution's final witness, forensic DNA scientist Laura Brown, to confirm.

***

Brown, also with the state police laboratory, did so, early in her testimony.

"The DNA profile obtained from the known reference sample from Gregory Scott Hopkins matches the DNA profile obtained from the sperm fraction of the stain from the nightgown top from Catherine Walsh," she testified in response to questioning from prosecuting attorney Smith, "and the known reference sample from Gregory Scott Hopkins also matched the partial DNA profile obtained from the non-sperm fraction of the stain from the nightgown top from Catherine Walsh, and additionally the profile from Gregory Scott Hopkins matches the DNA profile obtained from the sperm fraction of the stain from the rope, item Q6M."

She was unable to obtain results from the bandana, its knot, or the fitted sheet, she testified. But she did obtain a partial DNA profile matching Hopkins' DNA from the seminal stain in the middle of the blue, flat sheet.

Her analyses eliminated three of the other original suspects – Ciccozzi, McGrail and Carlo. And she confirmed previous testimony that while DNA evidence can become degraded over the years, the degradation "does not change the DNA that is found. It just changes the amount of DNA and the amount of areas of the DNA that we can use to compare to an individual."

On cross-examination, Brown again confirmed for Ross that DNA analysis cannot be used to determine when and how the DNA was deposited.

Brown then offered new evidence in response to Ross' questioning regarding probability statistics – evidence that actually bolstered the prosecution's case because of the overwhelming probability of the match being Hopkins' DNA rather than someone else's.

Ross: "Could you talk about the statistics of the match on the nightgown versus the match to the robe tie?"

Brown: "Sure. The probability, this is in reference to the sperm fraction of the stain from the nightgown top, Item Q3M, and for this particular profile the probability of randomly selecting an unrelated individual exhibiting this combination of DNA types is approximately one in one-point-six quintillion from the Caucasian population, one in twenty-three quintillion from the African-American population, and approximately one in two-point-eight quintillion from the Hispanic population."

However, the probability for the sperm

fraction on the tie cord, she testified, was approximately 1 in 2.2 billion from the Caucasian population, 1 in 1.3 billion from the African-American population, and approximately 1 in 1.82 billion from the Hispanic population.

Hopkins is Caucasian.

Ross: "So there's no doubt Mr. Hopkins' DNA is there; is that right?"

Brown: "Yes, there is a match to his DNA."

Ross: "Can you tell how it was deposited?"

Brown: "No."

Ross: "Can you tell when it was deposited?"

Brown: "No."

Ross: "Can you tell if both locations were deposited at the same time?"

Brown: "No."

Brown confirmed for Ross that the concentration of DNA on the nightgown top was twice that of the tie cord.

Ross moved on to the sheet evidence and asked Brown if she had seen the report of his expert, Perlin, in which Perlin "found that there was evidence of Scott Walsh's DNA in the middle portion of the sheet and in the top right corner of the sheet."

"I have seen his report," she responded.

Asked if she had seen in Perlin's report his finding of evidence "of an unknown third person on the robe that he could not identify," she responded in the affirmative.

No follow-up testing or submission of this evidence to CODIS was made for either the sheet or the robe.

The prosecution having rested with Brown's testimony, Ross would revisit these areas – reliability of the evidence, thoroughness of the investigation, the possibility of another perpetrator, among other issues – more fully in the defense portion of the trial and in his summation.

But first, he wanted to establish the character of his client along with his alibi, provided by two friends and a female companion, all of whom said they spent the night and the following day with him at his model home on the evening before and the day of the murder.

The refutation of the scientific evidence –

including an unanticipated, surprising development regarding that evidence – would wait until the last day of the trial.

8

The chief task of attorney James Ross, as the trial moved into the defense phase, would be to demonstrate the good character of his client and, on the first day of defense witnesses testimony, to establish Scott Hopkins' alibi the evening prior to and the early morning of the murder, along with his version of the events of that time period.

And, in the attorney role reversal, it would now be the prosecuting attorneys' chore to poke holes in the defense witness' testimony – to raise doubts about the veracity of the alibi witnesses and, especially, of Hopkins himself.

***

The primary alibi testimony of that Monday afternoon of the trial would be a strong argument that it would have been difficult for Hopkins to commit the murder at the established time of the death – 4 to 5 a.m. This testimony came from Larry Musgrave, Hopkins' business associate in 1979, and from Musgrave's wife of 44 years, Georgeann Musgrave.

Musgrave and Hopkins were volunteer firemen for Economy Borough when they met in the early '70s, Musgrave testified, when Hopkins was married to his first wife, Ellen Hopkins. The two couples became fast friends, vacationing together, and after Musgrave quit Stylex Homes, a modular home manufacturer, Hopkins hired Musgrave to oversee office operations for Colony Square Builders. He appointed Musgrave secretary/treasurer of the company.

When Hopkins separated from his wife, in 1978 or 1979, Musgrave testified, Hopkins moved into the company's split-level model home in Center Township, staying in a back bedroom of the main upstairs floor. The rest of the home remained unfurnished. The basement served as the company office and was furnished with office fixtures. The only way in and out of the house, Musgrave testified, was down the main steps to the front door, down to the basement and through the garage – or through a sliding door that led to a back ground-level deck off the basement office.

Musgrave testified that on the Friday evening prior to the murder, he, Hopkins and a couple of company workers went waterskiing on the Ohio River from 6 to 8 p.m. After that, Musgrave, his wife, Hopkins and Hopkins' girlfriend, Dianne St. George, planned to spend the night at the model home preparing for a pig roast for Colony Square employees and families at the model home the next day. The group wanted to stay at the model home because Musgrave and Hopkins wanted an early start to "get the pig roasted and be, have it done, by noon," Musgrave testified.

Georgeann Musgrave and St. George met the men at the model home about 8:30 p.m., after the two women got off their jobs at the two banks where they worked. They were joined for picnic preparations that evening by another company employee and his wife, but that couple left the model home that Friday evening. Musgrave and his wife slept on the living room floor, Hopkins and St. George in Hopkins' bedroom on a waterbed, Musgrave testified.

Asked if the group consumed any alcohol that Friday evening, Musgrave said "possibly," adding that he did not drink that night. The party broke up around midnight or 1 Saturday morning, he said, and the two couples went to bed. He and Hopkins planned to get up at 5:30 or 6 a.m. to start the fire for the pig roast, he testified.

To get out of the house, it would have been necessary for Hopkins to cross the living room to get to the front door, the garage door in the basement, or the sliding glass door in the basement's back office. Musgrave said he did not hear a phone ring that evening.

Ross asked Musgrave if he recalled hearing anyone come down the hall and go down the steps.

"No, I did not," Musgrave testified.

The driveway was made of limestone, the witness testified, and "any vehicle you would hear driving on any type of a lime, I don't care if it would be a car or a truck. You would hear it on limestone, because it's not, it's just, you spin when you start out sometimes. It just makes noise under your tires."

Ross: "Did you hear any such noise that night?"

Musgrave: "No, sir."

Ross: "Did you ever hear any garage door go up at that house to reflect that someone may have even taken a vehicle out of the bottom garage?"

Musgrave: "Definitely not."

Ross: "Throughout the night did you ever hear the front door open?"

Musgrave: "No."

Ross: "Did you hear anybody leave the residence?"

Musgrave: "No, I did not."

Ross: "Did you hear anybody come back in?"

Musgrave: "Again, no, I did not."

Musgrave recalled that when he got up between 5:30 and 6 a.m. the next day, he saw Hopkins. His friend, he said, appeared "completely normal, wanted to get up and get going, get the fire started." Hopkins did not appear nervous or shaken.

Hopkins was there the entire morning as they started the fire and began the pig roast, Musgrave testified. The guests were scheduled to arrive beginning at about noon, and the pig roast "went fine," Musgrave testified.

Then, later in the day, Hopkins came to Musgrave and told him "he had to go to the police station ... he said there was a homicide." Hopkins told Musgrave that Janet Walsh had been killed.

"At that time did you know whether Mr. Hopkins had any involvement with Janet Walsh up to that day?" Ross asked.

"Did not know," Musgrave responded; but he did learn of the relationship later.

Hopkins, Musgrave said, left the party to talk to the police, and when he returned he spoke with Musgrave and "seemed surprised, but fine because he knew he wasn't involved."

The police interviewed Musgrave five or six days later. Hopkins did not seem concerned about this, said Musgrave, who left the company the next year during a slow period but remained good friends and a business partner with Hopkins in other ventures to the present day.

The police interviewed Musgrave again a few years after the murder, and then in 2011 he got a phone call, "asking if I would come up and talk to the state police and they wanted to speak to my wife at the same time, and I asked them in regards to what and they said they were re-investigating, re-opening the homicide case for Janet Walsh and they wanted to talk to me again. I said, 'Sure.' "

Musgrave signed a statement attesting to being with Hopkins that night, that he did not believe it was possible that Hopkins could have left the residence, and that he and Hopkins had taken turns turning the pig on the spit.

Ross: "Did you mean that you took turns turning the pig all night?"

Musgrave: "No sir."

Ross: "When did you take turns turning the pig?"

Musgrave: "In the morning after we started the fire."

Musgrave next heard from the police the night they arrested Hopkins. They came to his house around 11 p.m.

"They said the reason for their visit is they wanted to make me aware that they had arrested Scott Hopkins and they did not want me to hear that on the news was what they said."

The police asked Musgrave's wife to leave the room and questioned Musgrave.

"They wanted to just talk to me," he testified. "And we spoke for quite a while, and they kept saying 'do you want to change your story, because we have arrested Scott and we have very, very hard evidence.'

"My question to them was, 'what's the hard evidence?' And they said they could not tell me what it was. I said, 'because I know he wasn't there' " – at the murder scene.

"Scott couldn't have been there for the time that they said that he was there because he did not leave the model home office where we were at that night.

"So," Musgrave continued, "the one officer took his packet of papers in a binder and threw them on my kitchen counter, and he says, 'you see that there?' I said, 'yep.' He said, 'the proof we have is as good as that setting there.' I told him that it's not possible, because I know where he was at."

The police were in his house for two-and-half to three hours, Musgrave said, adding that he was asked if he wanted to change his story "multiple times."

Ross: "What did you repeatedly reply to them?"

Musgrave: "That there was not a story. It's how it actually happened. We were together all night and all morning and all of the next day."

His wife came back into the room, Musgrave said, "and I think she agreed with me that at that point that we needed to no longer speak, because they just kept going over and over and over the same thing."

By the time of a January of 2012 meeting with police, Musgrave had spoken with the police four times, he testified. He never changed his version of the events of that night and morning.

In his cross-examination, prosecuting attorney Martocci questioned Musgrave about his activities immediately following Hopkins' arrest, including Musgrave making several phone calls to people Musgrave and Hopkins knew, including pig-roast attendees.

Martocci asked Musgrave if he was acting as an advocate for Hopkins by making these calls, and, "in fact, the date of his arrest while you were there at your house and the police showed up, the defendant called you within about an hour to two hours of his arrest, isn't that true?"

"That is correct," Musgrave replied.

Martocci: "He called you right then and there while the police were there, right?"

Musgrave: "Yes."

Martocci asked Musgrave if he had ever gone over the alibi story with Hopkins.

Musgrave: "No."

Martocci: "You never talked about it with the defendant?"

Musgrave: "No."

Martocci: "Never?"

Musgrave: "No."

Martocci: "Not one time you never talked

about your alibi with the defendant himself, that's what you're telling this jury today?"

Musgrave: "No. Okay. I would talk about it some time, but most of every, all of my conversation has been with the investigating team (hired by Hopkins and Ross) and also with attorney Ross."

Musgrave testified that he had one meeting with a hired investigator from the Hopkins team, and he confirmed that after state police and detectives tried to talk to him on January 29, 2012, he refused to give any more information.

"Why did you hire an attorney then to represent you and refuse to talk to any of the police involved in this case?" Martocci asked. "You did hire an attorney, right?"

Musgrave: "Yes, I did."

Martocci: "Yet you have nothing to hide?"

Musgrave: "That is correct."

Martocci then turned his attention to the events leading up to the time of the murder, asking Musgrave about Hopkins' relationship with Janet Walsh. The prosecutor was curious how Musgrave could claim not to have known about

Hopkins' relationship with Janet Walsh when they had all had drinks together on social occasions. Hopkins had told police when he was initially interviewed on September 1, 1979, that he had gone to builders' meetings with Janet Walsh, Musgrave and Margie Farinacci at the Beaver Falls Holiday Inn.

"We went to the builders' meeting, Scott and I alone, and after the builders' meeting sometimes Margie Farinacci would show up for a drink after the meeting."

Martocci: "So you were seeing Margie at that time then?"

Musgrave: "No, sir."

Martocci: "And you knew at that time that the defendant was with Dianne St. George after leaving his first wife for Dianne St. George, right?"

Musgrave: "He was dating her, yes."

Martocci: "And did you know that he was also seeing Janet Walsh then?"

Musgrave: "Did not know that."

Turning his questioning to the overnighter at the model home before the pig roast, Martocci wondered how Musgrave could remember not sleeping well but not recall on what he had slept, whether it was on a blanket or a sleeping bag. Also, Martocci elicited testimony from Musgrave that now he could not remember if he had been drinking that day.

Moving to the January 29, 2012 report of the police visit to Musgrave following Hopkins' arrest, Martocci focused on Musgrave's precise language concerning whether Hopkins could have left the house undetected during the early morning hours of September 1, in which, according to the report, "Musgrave stated that this would not have been impossible, but it would have been impracticable."

"So," Martocci said, "it would not have been impossible for, looking at that map of the house again, for the defendant to just go out of that house and during that four and a half to five hour period of sleep time ..."

Musgrave: "No, that's not what I meant."

What he meant, Musgrave said, is that "everything in this world is possible," but it was not practical that Hopkins could have slipped out of the house unnoticed early the morning of September 1.

But a more troubling language discrepancy in Musgrave's statements and testimony had drawn Martocci's attention. Just when were Musgrave and Hopkins roasting the pig – beginning at 5:30 or 6 a.m. that Saturday, or much earlier than that?

Martocci read back to Musgrave his 2011 statement to the police, in their re-investigation of the case: " 'I slept there all night in the living room. Scott and I took turns rotating the pig on the outside fire for the employees to eat on Saturday.' "

Musgrave: "Right. That was a mistake. I said that earlier. That was incorrect. We got up at 5:30 in the morning to start that."

Martocci: "But when you wrote that in there on, in 2011 …"

Musgrave: "Yes."

Martocci: "… Okay, you didn't realize that was a mistake then, you realized that was a mistake later, isn't that right?"

Musgrave: "Well, the day I wrote that I

didn't realize …"

Martocci: "You didn't believe it was wrong then when you wrote it then, did you?"

Musgrave: "I miswrote it."

Martocci: "Okay. But when you read this, if any average person would read this, it would read that you and the defendant took turns over the course of the night, which would be indicated by the words 'all night,' by getting up at night and rotating this pig to be ready for Saturday? If somebody would read that, you would agree that is what they would think?"

Musgrave: "I agree, but that's not what I said happened back, five days after it happened in 1979." Nor, he said, did he say that later. "That was an incorrect, I wrote that incorrectly."

Martocci: "Right. In 2011 that's what you wrote. At the time you wrote it in 2011, you did not believe it was incorrect, because right there on the bottom it says that you're saying that that's true …"

Musgrave: "Yes."

Martocci: "By signing your name there?"

Musgrave: "Yes, I did. But I wrote it incorrectly, and I am certainly, if you look at the penmanship and the writing ability, I was not a writer."

Martocci: "Okay. I'm not asking if you were a writer or not. You believed then that this was the truth, you signed it; right?"

Musgrave: "Yes."

Martocci asked Musgrave if he had talked to Hopkins since signing that 2011 statement.

"Yes," the witness replied.

Upon further questioning, Musgrave now recalled that he had met with a member of Hopkins' investigating team twice rather than the once to which he had previously testified, and that during that second meeting he and the investigator, Jeff Bowman, agreed that Musgrave's 2011 statement about roasting the pig "all night" had to be corrected.

Martocci asked if Musgrave had called the police, or Detective Gall, to let them know about that mistake.

Musgrave: "No, I did not. I didn't realize I wrote it that way."

Martocci: "Of course you did, because you

spoke with their (Hopkins') investigating team and you told them that, but you refused to tell us any of that, right?"

Musgrave: "I never met with you after that."

Martocci: "Right. Because you refused ..."

Musgrave: "How could I tell you ..."

Martocci: "Because you refused to, because you hired your lawyer and you refused to take part in anything else other than talking with Mr. Bowman and fixing your statements that you made prior to 2012?"

Musgrave: "I refused to talk to yins any longer, because yins kept trying to talk me into changing ..."

The conflicting stories of just when Musgrave and Hopkins began roasting the pig would arise again when Musgrave's wife took the stand.

After confirming her husband's story about the events of the evening before and morning of the murder – including telling the court that she was a light sleeper because of a sick child and would have heard anybody walking in or out of the model home after everyone had gone to bed

– Georgeann Musgrave, under questioning from Ross' defense colleague Charles F. Bowers III, confirmed that she also had signed a statement that Hopkins and her husband had turned the pig spit all night.

"But to me five-thirty in the morning, five in the morning, that's the middle of the night to me. I'm not up at that time, so to me that's the middle of the night."

After learning from Georgeann Musgrave that she did not know of her husband meeting Margie Farinacci for drinks after builders' meetings at the Holiday Inn, Martocci bee-lined to the statement regarding the hours of tending the spit.

The statement, Martocci said to the witness, was "remarkably similar to what your husband wrote about he and the defendant getting up over the course of the night to get up to rotate the pig, and you went as far as to say that that was going on all evening on August thirty-first of 1979. That's what it says in your statement, correct?"

"Correct," Georgeann Musgrave replied.

So. Martocci wondered, was what she

wrote in her original statement inaccurate?

"All evening to me, like I said, they started the pig at around five. Five to me is the middle of the night," she said.

Was she aware, Martocci asked, that Hopkins in his statement to the police said that the two men had not begun cooking the pig until around 7:30 a.m? He asked her if she knew that.

"No, I didn't," she responded.

Martocci: "So you would consider seven-thirty to be in the morning, right?"

Georgeann Musgrave: "Not necessarily. I'm not up at seven-thirty."

Martocci: "So you don't consider seven-thirty the morning. You consider that the night?"

Georgeann Musgrave: "I still consider myself I was sleeping."

But, Martocci asked, was she up early with her husband and Hopkins, around six a.m., preparing for the picnic?

Georgeann Musgrave: "Right. I don't know what time I got up exactly."

Martocci: "Right. Just like you don't know when Hopkins left that house that night, isn't that right?"

Georgeann Musgrave: "No, sir."

Martocci asked if her statement regarding when the pig had been turned had changed after meeting with Bowman in 2012.

"Correct," she replied.

And, Martocci asked, did she not also bring up several other points of information, including the waterbed in Hopkins' bedroom, lack of air conditioning, graveled driveway in 2011, that she then included in an interview with Jeff Bowman at his offices on February 16, 2012?

"Correct," she affirmed.

Martocci then asked her about a later meeting with Bowman, on July 3 of 2012, when the subject was the November 2, 2011 statement regarding the hours of the pig-turning.

Martocci: "And then you told Mr. Bowman that what you wrote about Larry and Scott took turns turning the spit for the pig all evening, you said that, it says, 'Georgeann also stated that she did not mean that they were up through the night?' "

Georgeann Musgrave: "Correct."

Martocci: "Okay. And that you put then later, 'everyone went to bed, and Larry and Scott got up early and started cooking the pig'?"

Georgeann Musgrave: "Right."

Martocci: "Then what, again what you wrote back in 2011, you made the exact same mistake that Larry made on those two statements, isn't that right?"

Georgeann Musgrave: "Apparently."

Martocci: "And then you revised that after talking with Mr. Bowman on February 24th and then you re-re-revised that on July 3, 2012; right?"

Georgeann Musgrave: "I guess."

***

The next day, Dianne St. George, Hopkins' girlfriend and overnight guest the evening prior to and the morning of the murder of Janet Walsh, confirmed much of what the Musgraves had testified – along with a strong dose of her personal life, including her relationship with Hopkins. And then there was that waterbed, where they slept and played together once both had left their spouses.

She'd begun to see the defendant in 1978 while still married to her husband. The two couples had socialized since first meeting at a wedding, and she and Hopkins became attracted to each other. They entered into an affair, and she left her husband and moved to Beaver. Hopkins also left his wife while seeing St. George.

Her recollection of the evening of August 31, 1979, was the same as that of the Musgraves – that they had all gone to bed late after making picnic preparations.

Asked by Ross if she remembered Hopkins getting out of the waterbed and leaving, she said no.

Ross asked her if she recalled the waterbed "waving or shaking as if someone had gotten up?"

"No," she replied.

She testified that it would not have been possible for Hopkins to leave that night "because I would have totally been aware of somebody getting out of that bed, but is it, but I mean I can't, you know, I mean is, what is one hundred percent certain, but I am convinced, I believe, that he was totally there with me all night."

Asked if, though now divorced from Hopkins, she still had financial interests that she shared with him, she said she, Hopkins, and the Musgraves still owned properties together. The amount of income generated from those properties, she told Martocci on cross-examination, was either $250 or $500 per month. "It could be two-fifty. I split my share with Scott."

Martocci asked St. George about a woman Hopkins had been seeing near the end of his marriage to St. George.

"I would say he was seeing her before I knew that he was seeing her," she testified.

"In other words," Martocci said, "he deceived you about that. He didn't tell you about that; right?"

St. George: "He did not."

Martocci: "That's how your relationship ended with him, though, was one of the reasons, wasn't it?"

St. George: "There were many reasons why it ended."

Going back to the summer of 1979, she was seeing Hopkins regularly, St. George testified, at his model home and sometimes at her home, which she shared with a daughter. Before September 1 of 1979, she did not know that he had been seeing Janet Walsh while still in a relationship with her, she testified. She learned about the affair the day of the pig roast, when Hopkins returned from the police department.

Martocci: "And he tells you that he was, Janet Walsh was killed, and he was seeing her, those are your words?"

St. George: "Okay."

Martocci: "That, I'm sorry, those are his words that he told you at the picnic, right?"

St. George: "I don't remember. Quite frankly it, it has been a very long time, and nobody asked me ever, you know, before."

Martocci asked her if she knew that Hopkins had initially told police that he wasn't dating Janet Walsh.

"I never saw the police report," she responded. "I never, I haven't seen anything."

Martocci then read to St. George notes

prepared by investigator Bowman following his February 16, 2012 interview with St. George, in which she indicated having no recollection of going to bed, " 'no recall of anything.' "

But she had told Detective Andrew Gall in a November 2011 interview, said Martocci, "that you're sure, you're certain, that the defendant couldn't have left the house that night while you were in the bed, you testified to that, do you remember that?"

St. George: "That I was certain?"

Martocci: "Right."

St. George: "I did not say I was, I would never, the only person I can be certain of, sir, is myself."

Martocci asked her about a report from November of 2011 based on a telephone interview with Detective Gall while she was living in South Carolina. After reading over the report, St. George testified that she had never admitted to drinking.

"I don't drink a lot. I am not a catch up kind of person … that is totally fabricated."

But according to the sentence in the report

before the drinking reference, Martocci said, St. George " 'cannot say for sure that Hopkins never left that house that night.' "

"What I am saying," St. George responded, "is I am ninety-nine percent positive. Yes, I can speak for myself. I can say I was there, but could, but cannot speak for anybody else ever saying that anybody always does something, never does something. I can only speak one hundred percent for myself."

Martocci then asked her if she had told Bowman in July of 2012 that she could not be a hundred percent positive about whether Hopkins had left the model home that night or the next morning.

"Only because of what I just said to you, that I can only be sure of what I do. I can never speak for somebody else one hundred percent of that someone always does something, never does something. I mean do I think he was there, absolutely. I think he was there. I do not think he left."

St. George also recalled telling Martocci, a couple of weeks before the trial, that she was a "world class sleeper." But, she said, "back then, when I had a four-year-old daughter, no, I was not."

Though her daughter was not there that night or morning, she said, "I never could sleep well there."

But, when she got up, Hopkins, she recalled, was already up.

"Had to do that pig."

That pig, that night, the affair with Janet Walsh – all would be the subject of the recollection of Scott Hopkins when he took the stand in a day that mixed testimony of remembrance of decades back with the science of modern day.

The science will be the opening subject of the next chapter, followed by Hopkins' tale.

9

Dr. Cyril Wecht's admonition regarding the decision by DNA analysts of evidence found at Janet Walsh's apartment not to test for anything but sperm was quite prescient. Seemingly prophetic, considering the testimony of a pathologist called to testify by the attorneys tasked with defending Scott Hopkins. Dr. Michael Panella, staff pathologist at Quest Diagnostics, a clinical laboratory services firm, told the court that "several issues" made him "cautious about just using the sole location of this DNA and the semen as proof of somebody's guilt or trying to recreate the position and when it was deposited."

Panella, who, like Wecht, also had a law degree and whose background included work as a hospital pathologist, and as a forensic pathologist at the Allegheny County Medical Examiner's office, based his comments on his review of Wecht's opinion statement, the autopsy and the state police laboratory reports.

"The first issue that I really have to question is, is that, are there other potential reasons for why that seminal DNA was deposited at those sites," testified Panella, who died a couple of months after the trial. "In my opinion, yes, there are."

These reasons included the fact of previous sexual encounters between Hopkins and Janet Walsh, when the semen that was analyzed could have been deposited. Or, he said, there was a possibility of indirect contact – that "after sex there might have been fresh semen deposits on either Mrs. Walsh or Mr. Hopkins' hands, body, that got in contact with those items" such as the bed sheets, nightgown or other items analyzed by the state lab.

Also, he said it was possible that when the articles were washed, "believe it or not, the semen, the sperm can actually lift off the contaminated garments that are being washed and deposit on the other pieces of the garments that have not been stained and then, now they are contaminated with sperm."

Finally, he posited the potential for cross-contamination, reasoning that police working the case in 1979 did not have an understanding of DNA. Thus, "it is easy potentially to have a moist stain that you might have brushed against and then you go and you touch another part of the scene and you transfer that semen onto the other part that you're now touching."

Jurors by now had become immersed in the DNA "classroom" that Ross had promised them in his opening statement, as Panella continued in his testimony to indicate that science indeed is open to interpretation, possible error, and even manipulation. Besides the possibility of tainted or transferred DNA, Panella gave the jury a quick lesson in sperm ejaculation – basically, when large amounts of sperm are ejaculated, it can and likely would be found in numerous other places besides the locations of the deposits analyzed for this case. He said there was no report, for example, of semen stains, "on the victim's skin or any grossly appearing stains on the bedding or on the rope tie, and was nothing that was present" in the autopsy analysis. "So that is another thing that makes me step back and view the location and trying to use that to precisely recreate the scene, and the timing gives me a lot of caution based on the science of semen."

Panella also found problems with the conclusions Wecht had drawn regarding the potential positioning of Hopkins on the victim's back in relation to where the sperm was deposited. And he raised the possibility of contamination caused by the urine and body movements when her body was turned over or when placing her into the autopsy bag. Also, cross-contamination was possible by police placing the flat and fitted sheets in the same evidence bag.

Finally, Panella expressed grave concerns about the same subject that had caused Wecht pause: those areas of staining that were not tested because they did not contain sperm. The binding cord, for example, had fluoresced in its entirety, "and that may indicate that that could potentially be, maybe the pigmentation of the rope. It could also be that there's other bodily fluids that are present, in addition to semen or maybe there's more semen stains present."

Also present on the cord, he testified, was "what is called the non-sperm fraction of the extract, they found not only, they found a mixture, and a mixture could be potentially other people's, would be consistent with other people's DNA that are present."

"So," Panella summarized, "that is another reason you have to step back and really question if you rely on DNA alone, in terms of identifying Mr. Hopkins and linking it at that time to the crime, you have to start to think and be careful, because now there's a third, potential third party."

And because of the length of time involved, more than three decades, DNA degradation should be considered.

"So, you know, you have to start to ask yourself," Panella testified, "is there other people's DNA potentially at a higher level that would have been detected if they had tested this back in the early '80s before the DNA started to degrade."

Moving now to the nightgown, Panella

conceded that the plus-four sperm finding there was a "fair amount … the most amount that you can see" so far as microscopic descriptions are considered, but he again had concern about the limitations of the areas tested.

"Unfortunately, in this case," he said, "the analysts did not look at another area submitted for analysis that had fluoresced to look and see if there was a mixture of somebody else's DNA."

Speaking to the untested areas, the doctor testified that he was troubled by the limitations of the state's findings.

"There is previous semen stains that are being transferred around. You know, that inability to have looked at these other things to see if they were bodily fluids, I think also makes me very skittish when you're starting to just base your whole process, your whole ability to link Mr. Hopkins to the time of Mrs. Walsh's death based on these areas of DNA alone from the, from sperm makes me very, very worried."

Panella voiced the same concerns regarding the sheets.

"So, once again, this whole case is based

on bodily fluids, DNA. That's the main bulk at least from what I can tell looking over the records, and for not to have gone through that and to see if there was saliva, other urine stains that may have linked somebody else to that scene, makes me, once again, very, very guarded in terms of the dogma of trying to opine that those semen stains alone at those sites matches Mr. (Hopkins), therefore, means he was on top of her at the time ..."

The doctor noted that this case marked the first time, of a total of fifteen cases, that he had ever testified for the defense and that first he had seen this as a "slam dunk case. But as I started to review and I started to think about it and the semen physiology, the significance of DNA, its limitations, cross-contamination, previous sexual encounter, that's why I'm testifying here today, because there are significant questions in this."

In cross-examination, after obtaining testimony indicating that Panella's experience in autopsies and forensics science (including no expertise in serology) was relatively less than Wecht's, prosecutor Smith asked Panella if his testimony regarding the potential of DNA transfer from the wet urine stain beneath Janet Walsh's body would be different if the urine-stained sheet had been dry.

"That would make the cross-contamination from the urine stain highly unlikely, not to say impossible, but highly unlikely," he responded.

Smith asked Panella if he recalled in his written case report discussing finding Hopkins' DNA on the bandana used to strangle Janet Walsh.

"Yes," the witness responded.

Smith: "– that there was no match to Mr. Hopkins on the bandana? Well, do you also recall that there's no match to anybody? There wasn't enough to draw a conclusion there, do you recall that?"

Panella: "I do, but that's the problem in terms of using this DNA is the degree of degradation and potential mixtures that may be occurring. We're talking thirty years later. How do we not know other people's DNA may be, may have been present? Because all throughout this, there is a lot of items that they tested insufficient DNA,

DNA degradation."

Later in the cross-examination, Panella disputed that the position of the body when it was found was necessarily its position at the time of death. He suggested that the body could have been put in that position after death – a suggestion that, if accurate, could completely undermine Wecht's theory of the killer's positioning during the strangulation.

"Suppose that she was strangled in an upright position and then is placed in that position by the perpetrator," he said. Viewing the photograph of the dead body and its position, Panella suggested that the urine stain could have been deposited later. All of which, of course, could throw into question Wecht's theory of how and thus when the sperm had been deposited.

"I just find it hard, based on that photograph alone and the information being provided, that I can say she died exactly in that position. I don't think that is possible."

The victim's laundry habits came under question. What about those four-plus stains, Smith wondered. Is such a strong finding possible if the garments had been washed? Could it be that she had not washed her nightgown in the three to four weeks since her last sexual encounter with Hopkins?

"We get busy," Panella responded. "I mean I, I don't, it's, is it an absolute habit that is always followed, who knows? God only knows."

"Wouldn't a guy have to be pretty darn unlucky to have his DNA on all of those places?" Smith asked.

"As I said before," Panella countered, "there are plausible explanations, and the fact that he has had previous encounters at that site and there's, there is the possibility of cross-contamination and there is the possibility of the previous encounters leading to the deposition of the semen at those sites, I mean I just don't have the degree of, reasonable degree of certainty to be able to say that based on the presence of Mr. Hopkins' DNA at that location that I can pinpoint him being on top of Mrs. Walsh at the time of death. I just don't."

Smith: "You would agree with me though that he would have to be pretty unlucky for his

DNA to be found at all three of those places?"

Panella: "Very unfortunate."

Those plausible explanations, the previous sexual encounters – all of this would be much of the focus of Hopkins' testimony when he took the stand later that day as the trial segued to less quantitative, more qualitative, evidence. His story of the events of the eve and that deadly morning would dominate the remaining testimony of the day, offering not only his version of events but also a study of character – his.

***

Defense attorney Ross brought up the infidelity issue.

After the preliminary questions establishing Hopkins' education (a year and a half at Point Park University, which was then a junior college, studying drafting), professional resume (various drafting and office work for different companies before founding Colony Square Builders following the completion and sale of his first modular home in 1974 or '75) and personal background (married to Ellen in 1967, two children and pregnant with the third when they separated in 1978), Ross asked Hopkins if he had started cheating on his wife around the time of the third pregnancy.

"Yes, I did," said the short, balding defendant. "I had met Dianne St. George at a real estate function, because I also had a real estate license at the time. Her husband worked with us. We worked in the same office, and through office and social events we met and I met her."

After the separation, Hopkins split time between his parents' house and the model home he and Musgrave had put up. St. George, he testified, was his "main" girlfriend then. He hired Margie Farinacci, whom he had met when his company built a home for her and her husband, to clean completed houses and prepare them for sale. It was through Margie that he met Janet Walsh, he testified.

Hopkins admitted that he developed a relationship with Janet Walsh – one of which he was not proud, he testified. Back then, he told the court, "I thought of myself as a virile young, a young man, and I probably did a lot of womanizing, and I'm not necessarily proud of it, but it, it is a fact."

He and Janet entered into a conversation about divorce – she was separated from her husband – and she invited him to her apartment.

"I went on several occasions over the summer of 1979. I don't know how many, but was, it was a few," he testified in an alteration from his original statement of seeing her only a couple of times.

"Sometimes she would call me, knowing that I was sleeping at the office, she would call me and ask me if I wanted to come down, and I would say, 'yes.' "

He would go late at night, he said, "and I would see her and we would just talk about things, you know, about what was going on in her life, what was going on in my life. We never actually went on any dates. We never had any kind of a social relationship other than I can remember several times that at a builders' meeting that were on Wednesday nights once a month that her and Margie Farinacci had stopped out one or two occasions and had a drink after the meeting was over with us. But when I was at the house, it ended up in a, in a sexual relationship."

Hopkins said Janet's estranged husband was jealous, "so she would always want me to park on a different street."

He would park about a block away and then go up the alley to her apartment and enter through the back door.

"Sometimes she had already gotten ready for bed. She had, you know, her nightgown on and her robe. She, you know, we would sit in the living room for a little bit and talk, and then we would go to bed."

Their sex, he testified, was normal.

"I think there's a term out there for what most of us think as normal sex as a missionary position which would be the woman facing up and the man facing down. And I think on occasions we had sex more than once in the evening," he said. "I was a lot younger then and there would be times that it would be, and I don't know the name of the term, but it would be, that she would be facing down and I would be on top of her."

These trysts, Hopkins said, lasted two to

three hours "at the most." Afterwards, he said, "sometimes we would just lay in bed and talk a little bit. It wasn't like, excuse my expression, wham bam, thank you, ma'am. We would talk, but I would always get up and, anywhere from probably one to two, and go back to my office, because I had to be back up in the morning around between six and seven, because I had employees coming and I needed to have them ready to go to work."

He kept the relationship secret, he said. "I wasn't ashamed of it, but I didn't think it was anybody else's business, and it was, it was just a sexual friendship."

Ross asked Hopkins about his activities of the day and evening before the murder.

Hopkins' story matched that of the Musgraves and St. George. He picked up the pig Friday afternoon, followed by waterskiing on the Ohio until about 8 p.m., then adjourning to the model home to prepare for the next day's company employee picnic. After employee Don Young and his wife left at eleven or midnight, the Musgraves, St. George and Hopkins stayed up until 1 a.m. or so.

When was the last time he'd talked to Janet Walsh, Ross asked.

Hopkins: "Probably about a week, week and a half previous."

Ross: "What kind of contact was that?"

Hopkins: "If I remember correctly I think that I had called her to see if she was interested in my coming down that night, and based on the statement that I wrote, and I've had a chance to read, I believe that she had told me she was already sleeping and let's make it another time."

Ross: "Prior to that it had been two or three weeks or so?"

Hopkins: "Several weeks before."

Hopkins testified that he had no knowledge of Janet's whereabouts the night preceding her death and had not received a phone call from her.

"Absolutely not," Hopkins answered Ross' question of whether he'd left the house that night.

He got up the next morning at 5:30 or 6 to start the fire, he said; it would take five to six hours to cook the 70-pound pig once it was on the fire. Margie Farinacci's husband, Joe, phoned Hopkins that afternoon to inform him that Margie had a "personal problem" and they could not attend the pig roast.

"I'm not sure there weren't two phone calls," Hopkins testified, "but my response to it was, " 'oh, I'm sorry to hear that.' Then I think Joe Farinacci told me that her girlfriend, and I can't remember how he said it, that he said she was murdered or that she had died the night before, and I just couldn't remember which way it was stated, and then I asked Joe is there anything I can do, and he said, 'no.' "

Later that day, the Monaca police contacted him, told him "they were investigating a situation and asked me if I could come down and talk to them."

He did so.

Ross: "And at first you were a little reluctant to tell them about Janet Walsh?"

Hopkins: "Sure."

Ross: "Why?"

Hopkins: "Well, I had a girlfriend, and I

really was concerned about how she was going to react to that."

Ross: "Did you eventually that day tell the police about your relationship?"

Hopkins: "Yeah, fairly, not first thing, but yes, fairly, fairly soon into the interview I did."

After returning to the pig roast, which had started to break up, he said he told St. George about his relationship with Janet later that evening.

Ross: "What did you tell her at that point?"

Hopkins: "I had told her that I had been having a sexual relationship with the girl that had been murdered."

Ross: "Mr. Hopkins, were you at 935 Indiana Avenue that early morning?"

Hopkins: "Absolutely not."

Ross: "Did you kill Janet Walsh?"

Hopkins: "Absolutely not."

Ross: "Once you told Dianne what happened, what was the reaction?"

Hopkins: "She was pissed off."

Ross: "What happened then?"

Hopkins: "Our relationship kind of, we

didn't stop seeing each other, but it cooled for a while. We weren't necessarily exclusive, but I had never discussed it with her and she had never asked me about it."

Asked if the police had questioned him again, Hopkins said yes, about three weeks later for a follow-up interview.

"At that point in time did you answer all of their questions?" Ross asked.

"I think I did."

Hopkins said he did not hear from the police again until the summer of 2011. Meanwhile, he testified that he had filed for bankruptcy for his company, but that he did not hide any of his assets during that proceeding. After a while, he re-entered the construction business building larger homes along with modulars, operated under his own name: Gregory S. Hopkins. And he began a snow-plow business to supplement his construction work. He and St. George married in 1983, a union that lasted until 1999.

While married to St. George, he testified, he became involved with another woman, "probably '92, '93, in that area."

This affair, he said, caused problems in his marriage to St. George, and they eventually separated. He then met and married his current wife, the former Karen Fisher. In 2004 or 2005, he testified, he was invited to join the Bridgewater Planning Commission, and then in 2010 was asked by the borough council to fill a council position that had become vacant. He was elected to the position in the fall of 2011, but resigned the post after being charged with killing Janet Walsh.

Then he got a call from Detective Andrew Gall asking him to come in for questioning. He met with law enforcement officials, including Rocco DeMaiolo of the state police, and "they explained to me they were opening a cold case. They said that they thought they had a suspect, and they were trying to work on developing evidence for that subject. But they were reviewing all of the people that had been contacted back then or was involved in the case."

In December of 2011, police took a buccal swab from Hopkins, and then he was arrested in January of 2012, he testified (the judge had, during pre-trial case proceedings, disallowed evidence and testimony regarding Hopkins' original refusal to provide a DNA sample and subsequent warrant ordering him to do so).

Ross: "Mr. Hopkins, did you have anything to do with the death of Janet Walsh, Catherine Janet Walsh on September first of 1979?"

Hopkins: "Absolutely not."

Prosecutor Martocci, in his cross examination, explored character and veracity issues, beginning with Hopkins' feelings about Janet Walsh – which, the defendant made clear, did not go beyond sexual desire.

Martocci began with a rhetorical question: "Janet Walsh, she meant nothing to you, isn't that right?"

That is an inaccurate statement, Hopkins replied.

"So you developed some kind of new-found affection for her after she was killed?" Martocci asked.

"No," Hopkins answered, adding that he had no emotional involvement with Janet. It was, he testified, a "casual relationship."

Martocci: "Just sex?"

Hopkins: "Basically, yes."

Asked if he had ever expressed sorrow over Janet Walsh's death, Hopkins responded, "no, I never made … any statements. I only responded to the questions I was asked."

Queried about his first statement to the police, that he didn't know Janet other than to talk to her, Hopkins parried with Martocci about the truthfulness of that initial response and then about a subsequent response to the same questioning regarding how well he knew Janet and how many times he had seen her – a couple of times, or four, five or six times.

"A couple depends on how you want to phrase it," Hopkins offered, adding that he would not agree that a couple means two to most people. He then conceded, after lengthy back-and-forth about how many times he'd seen Janet and how well he knew her, that it wasn't until after repeated questioning by police that he finally admitted that he knew her and had sex with her: "Sure."

Conceding that his relationship with Janet was secret, Hopkins then confirmed that so far as he knew, she did not have a sexual relationship with anybody else during the few weeks before her death. He repeated that he had not told St. George about the relationship with Janet which, so far as he knew, was still ongoing at the time of her death. He also testified that he had met Janet, along with Musgrave and Margie Farinacci, "several" times at the Holiday Inn following Wednesday night builders' meetings.

Martocci then turned his attention to the model home where Hopkins was staying the morning of the murder. He asked if Hopkins had allowed his employees to use the model home for sexual trysts.

"I would assume being an adult that they were intending to have sex, yes," Hopkins testified.

Martocci then asked Hopkins if he kept Polaroid camera snapshots of naked women to share with company employees.

"I have no recollection of that," Hopkins replied.

"Just another one of those things that you don't remember from 34 years ago, right?" Martocci asked.

"Yep," Hopkins responded.

Martocci asked Hopkins to elaborate on his sexual relations with the victim. Hopkins told the court that he and she had used the missionary position and that he had also entered her from the back.

Martocci: "And during these sexual encounters you ejaculated, right?"

Hopkins: "I would hope so."

Martocci: "You think this is funny?"

Hopkins: "I'm not laughing."

Martocci: "What about ejaculating on her back, how many times did you do that?"

Hopkins: "I do not recall any times."

Moving on to the day of the arrest, and the days after, Martocci was curious if Hopkins had conversed with Musgrave after he was arrested.

Hopkins said he had, but primarily about business and not about the case. "We were still trying to run a business without me there," he testified.

Asked if he knew that Musgrave was making telephone calls to St. George and company employees about the case on Hopkins' behalf, the defendant said he didn't know about that.

Asked if he had developed a relationship with another woman while married to St. George, Hopkins responded, "Yes, I did." Furthermore, he testified, he had met with that other woman and a girlfriend of hers at his house one afternoon about six or seven months before the trial, in the absence of his current wife, and had discussed the case with her.

"And again this is one of your old girlfriends that you met with at your house without her there, and in fact, (the other woman) wanted to kind of get out of there before your present wife got home, isn't that right?" Martocci asked.

"No, that's not correct," responded Hopkins.

Martocci: "But she wasn't there, was she, your present wife?"

Hopkins: "No."

Martocci then asked Hopkins about another relationship he'd had, "and that relationship ended partly because you began seeing other women?"

"Partly, yes," Hopkins answered.

After more questions about Hopkins' various relationships over the years, Martocci asked Hopkins if he would agree, "that that string of people that you have been with, you weren't truthful and honest with them, were you?"

"Probably not," Hopkins replied.

Martocci then moved to the crux of his character testimony, asking if "every relationship that we know of that you have had in this case has been the result of deceit and lies?"

"I would agree with that," Hopkins responded.

Martocci: "So over 34 years, Mr. Hopkins, you have become accustomed to living lies, is that not accurate?"

Hopkins: "A good portion of those years probably, yes."

Martocci: "A good portion of the years, how about all those years?"

Hopkins: "No."

During recross examination, Martocci asked Hopkins what he knew about the upcoming testimony of the defense's star expert DNA witness, Dr. Mark Perlin, and what was found at the scene of the murder.

Your witness, Martocci said, "confirms what the state police found and where your DNA is found at that scene, right?"

Hopkins: "I believe that's correct."

Martocci: "So not only are you the only person who had been there making late-night visits that we heard about so far, your own witness, Dr. Perlin, is going to say that your DNA through seminal fluid is the only DNA that is found on the middle of her back and on that rope that binds her hands, you know he's going to say that; right?"

Hopkins: "I believe that's correct."

Martocci asked Hopkins if he had any explanation for how his DNA was found on Janet Walsh's nightgown or on the tie cord.

Not other than from previous sexual relationships, Hopkins responded.

The details of that DNA evidence would come during the highly anticipated testimony of Dr. Mark Perlin the next day when science would again take center stage in a high-tech rendering analyzing not so much what was found in terms of DNA. Rather, a computer analysis of just what story this DNA evidence can or – often just as meaningful – perhaps cannot tell about this crime would be the focus of Perlin's testimony.

10

If Dr. Michael Panella had served as the palliative anti-Dr. Cyril Wecht, then Dr. Mark Perlin would be the intended outright antidote to Wecht. The trial concluded by moving into the senior capstone portion of defense attorney James Ross' promised DNA "classroom," with testimony designed to negate the damage done by Wecht's testimony for the prosecution. Perlin's DNA analysis would highlight the conclusion of the trial, followed by the attorneys' closing arguments and jury deliberation.

The testimony of Perlin, the chief executive officer and chief scientific officer of Cybergenetics, a 20-year-old Pittsburgh firm, specializing in computer analysis of DNA evidence, spun off from Pittsburgh's Carnegie Mellon University, would offer a stark departure from the DNA analysis presented by the state's crime lab, by Wecht, and even by Panella.

Perlin, a licensed medical doctor of about 20 years before allowing his license to lapse, said his company relies on a technology called TrueAllele, in which electronic genetic data from crime labs is fed to a computer.

The computer, he explained, "thinks about the problem for a few hours, a few days, or a few weeks, depending on how complex the problem is, if there's two, three, or four different people it interprets, and then when it's done, the computer then produces a genetic type or a genotype that can be compared against other individuals."

About fifteen years prior, he explained, his company had developed software to automate genetic testing interpretations on a genetic marker used to detect disease and then to make a genetic diagnosis of it "so that people didn't have to read the data with a high error rate, and computers can read it with virtually no errors or mistakes."

The technology was used to eliminate a backlog of thousands of genetic reference samples from criminals for the FBI and has been used in Britain and by several states in the U.S., testified Perlin, who also has a Ph.D. in computer science from Carnegie Mellon University. His researchers, he testified, had published numerous articles focusing on how to use the data his company produces and, more recently, "how you can make more use of the computer to interpret harder and harder data questions, say, with five contributors at a very low level that are beyond what people can do" with other methods. Also, he testified, he wrote a chapter, titled "DNA Identification Science, an Introduction for Lawyers," for Wecht's book, "Forensic Sciences," and he had lectured for the Wecht Institute and served on an advisory board for the institute. He had testified in courts in the United States, and in Ireland, and several times in criminal trials for the prosecution, but this was the first time he had ever testified as an expert witness for the defense, he said.

Forensic scientists, he said, "asked us, 'what could we do about evidence,' which was much more of a problem, like mixtures of two or more people, degraded DNA, low levels of

DNA, and we began working on technology that used much more sophisticated math and computing and advanced statistics in order to solve that problem and resolve the uncertainties that are inherent in evidence data, as opposed to cheek swabs, which are very simple reference samples." His company, he testified, had worked with DNA exclusively since 1994. The concept behind the TrueAllele system, he told the jury, "is that numerous methods have been developed, that instead of trying to say yes or no, they look – they evaluate all the possible solutions that can be written down, and by carefully examining what the different alternative hypotheses are, different solutions, they can explain the data to derive a solution, making it more concrete."

What the computer does, he added, is examine the data, "spends maybe a day trying out a hundred-thousand different possibilities. When it's done, it discusses, 'what are the better explanations,' determines what the probabilities of each answer is, and then it stops and says, 'here is an objective genotype, one for each of the people who may have contributed to the DNA,' without any bias, knowing what the answer might be. 'This is what the DNA is telling us.'

"Then after it stops doing that, afterwards, comparisons can be made against the genetic types, eliminations of individuals or suspects or anyone you want to compare it against with a DNA match statistic."

The sort of computer analysis he uses helps eliminate human bias of interpretation, he said.

"People tend to cherry pick when they are doing a manual review without using a sophisticated computer, and if, where they can make a call, they'll use a lot less data," he testified. "For example, if the match statistic is really on the level of a trillion, they might report a million, but if the level is more at the level of a million, then the review might report nothing at all, and so the problem that's been developing was true at the time and has probably gotten even worse because more interesting evidence is being submitted by the police to crime labs, and that at this point, most of the evidence in many of the crime labs – probably all of the ones that I have worked with

– are mixtures, and most of them are not interpretable, and so what's happening is that if you don't use computers, a better microscope to look at the same data that a person is looking at, but with far more math and computing sophistication, that evidence is just discarded.

"It's not used, it's under-interpreted, and for all the effort that went into collecting the evidence, it never makes it into the criminal justice system as genotypes or genetic data."

And in a further explanation that would be key in this trial, he testified that the problem with the use of DNA threshold statistics concerns levels that come in under a predetermined level and tend to be discarded.

"And so we are involved in a lot of cases where the informative data about – that are not about the victims, but about the people who might be more of interest, are just not used." Thus, he concluded that in this case, "the amount of DNA does matter."

Tossing out some of the data, he said, "or keeping it based on a single line is converting very information-rich quantitative data into very information-poor or no-data-at-all data patterns, and so the problem is the loss of information that a computer can extract quantitatively that a person cannot do qualitatively."

In other words, discarding some of the DNA evidence for threshold-level or other reasons places too much reliance on human factors of interpretation that can be open to bias or error and too little on more objective empirical, unbiased analysis.

Moving to the specifics of this particular case, Perlin testified that he had used electronic data, pertaining to all of the evidence items from the scene, provided by the state's crime lab. These items were then analyzed by scientists at his lab using digital software on the computers at their stations.

All of the genotypes from the various items – labeled Q and K, for example – were compared against those of other items, "and then that comparison can be represented in a data table where we can see what the strength of the match is, and, for example, if the strength of match is a million, because a million has six zeroes in it, we put a six, or the computer will put a six in the entry form, say, this particular Q and that particular K.

"If the number is a blank," he said, "it means that there was no positive association. If the number is three, three zeroes, a thousand. Fifteen would be quadrillion as the number, and so by looking at the magnitude of the number, we get a sense of, where is the strength of the match between evidence items and the knowns?"

Ross had some tables displayed for the court and asked Perlin to use the tables to explain his findings. The witness began with the handkerchief, or bandana that was used in the strangulation and said his computer analysis found "no positive association to anyone involved as a known suspect in the case of the handkerchief, and the same with the fingernails."

The computer analysis, he said, found a "strong positive association to the defendant of fifteen zeroes" on the nightgown top, "which is number up in the quadrillions, which indicates that the defendant's DNA matched to the stain found on the nightgown top. On the bathrobe cord, there was also a strong, reasonably strong association of seven zeroes, which is ten million, and that would indicate that the defendant, it was his DNA stain on the bathrobe cord."

However, the analysis of a blue bathrobe found at the crime scene revealed a split of male and female DNA contributors, "and there was a clear second contributor. It was a degraded sample so that you lose signal. You really lose some. There was clearly a second contributor," he testified. This genotype, he said, "belongs to someone other than any of the suspects who were tested, that if you found that right person, and you actually found the person who contributed that DNA, the expected value would be in the order of a billion."

DNA of another person also was found on the top sheet – the DNA of Scott Walsh, Perlin testified. But it was a low number.

Ross asked Perlin to explain for the jury how his findings differed from those of the state lab.

Conceding that his computerized findings verified the state's findings of high levels of Hopkins' DNA on the nightgown top, on the robe tie cord used to bind her hands, and on the bed sheet, Perlin told the court that the computer finding of DNA on a portion of the blue bathrobe of nine zeros, or a billion, was significant.

"That's a possible lead in the case," Perlin testified, indicating "that not only is there another possible lead that could be explored, to look for a person who might have been there, or whatever theory the police may have had for why they were looking at this area in the first place, but – but it also indicates that there's DNA in areas that don't have sperm … that suggests that there could be more probative DNA for people who might not be expected to have been there or left their DNA there in other areas of a crime scene that could be probably examined."

Perlin then delivered the crux of the defense argument concerning "sampling bias," or analyzing only the evidence samples containing sperm.

"I found it surprising that they only were looking for semen and sperm in a case where a – a young woman had had multiple partners and previous sexual activity," he testified, "because that would have been expected to be there, and what you would be finding is more and more evidence of previous sexual activity, as opposed to something that might be related to her death."

Asked about the nearly one hundred sample areas that produced fluorescence but were disregarded, Perlin responded that "if the police were looking for a suspect, then DNA testing on those hundred areas might help them find someone who left their DNA for some reason other than prior sexual activity." The investigators, he suggested, possibly ignored "what may be the real probative evidence, because anything you'd find in a semen stain would typically not be surprising. You would expect to find evidence of prior sexual activity matching specific people when you know there's prior sexual activity, so it's – it's less – less. It's not probative, and it's – it's not – if you were looking for something related to a death, and you know there is prior sexual activity, you'd probably be spending your time looking at non sperm, non semen."

Ross then moved on to the question of

possible transfer of DNA.

Direct transfer is possible, Perlin testified, when it becomes wet, for example. "It can get on people's hands. It can then be redeposited. It's – um, semen tends to go everywhere, and sperm cells are – are very tiny. They are basically the most – about the most dense DNA packages that exist, so if you have sperm cells, as opposed to other cells, you will have a lot more concentrated DNA in one area."

DNA transfer, Perlin testified, can happen between wet surfaces, porous surfaces, such as certain fabrics like cotton, and DNA can flow upwards "from one surface to another."

Having laid this foundation, Ross opened the door to the possibility of DNA transfer through perspiration, such as the sweat that might occur from the exertion of the heart during strangulation. He asked Perlin to speculate on such a possibility.

Another explanation of the events known of that morning, Perlin testified, "might be that you have a – a victim who's – who's being, um, strangled, she's sweating, and as she sweats, um, the clothing that she's wearing, which in this case is a single layer cotton polyester nightshirt, becomes wet. If a – a semen stain had been deposited sometime earlier onto that nightshirt, then as that cloth material becomes wet, and as we saw from the photos, her hands are bound behind her and is creating pressure from the robe tie up against the nightshirt, you have the exact conditions that are ideal for – for semen or DNA transfer, so if semen had been deposited before the time of death, left on a nightshirt in any one of innumerable ways, then over subsequent time, weeks or months, that become invisible, less visible than it had been, that it rolled, or it got wet with moisture – possibly it had been washed or rinsed – and the semen stain is no longer visible."

However, he explained, as the nightshirt dampens with sweat, and as the robe tie exerts pressure against it, "like a spring action of the – of the arms up against the back, creating pressure, you expect some transfer of those sperm cells to the cotton fabric, from the cotton polyester nightshirt to the cotton robe tie just like capillary action. Capillary action is when – it's like, again, if you put a towel down on the floor, the water rises into it from the surface.

"In fact, if you wait long enough, you'll get an equal amount in both – in both, um, materials, and so it flows in over time, and she's moving, and she's struggling, as we heard Dr. Wecht say – this isn't instantaneous – previously-left semen can move from – through the moisture and the pressure from the nightshirt up into the robe tie, and then at a later time, eight hours later, say, when a police investigator arrives, there's now invisible semen that's been transferred from a previously-left DNA stain on a nightshirt into a robe tie, and the reason the transfer occurred is that they were located in the same place."

His scenario was just as likely as that of Wecht, if not more so, Perlin said, "given the additional fact that somehow the semen managed to miss all the skin.

"If you bring in the additional fact that the stains are invisible on the back – on the back of the blue nightshirt, the semen stains aren't visible on the cotton robe tie, and the stains are invisible on both of the – of the bed sheets, semen stains, um, I would find it extremely unlikely that a trained police investigator, a trained pathologist, a trained coroner, and a trained criminologist at a crime lab would all miss four semen stains that would otherwise be visible."

Perlin concluded: "Given that Mr. Hopkins had been there before, um, and had sexual activity, I would think the probative – the probative evidence of DNA found on clothing and on sheets, not found in a rape kit, not found on the handkerchief or something associated with the manner of death, for anyone who had previous sexual activity would not be probative as a reason why it's there. There's no surprise … I think there's no probative DNA evidence that's been presented in this case."

***

But prosecutor Martocci, in his cross-examination, would claim probative DNA evidence not only in the findings of the state lab but, ironically, in Perlin's computer-generated analysis of the state's DNA evidence. First, though, Martocci wanted to make a few points clear to the jury. One was that Perlin's company analyzed electronic data only and did not look at the linens, clothing or other items themselves. And he questioned Perlin's credentials and method.

Martocci: "You don't do autopsies, do you?"

Perlin: "No, not that I ..."

Martocci: "You are not a forensic pathologist, right?"

Perlin: "That's true. I am an expert on DNA, not a forensic pathologist."

Martocci: "Now, you mentioned something just towards the end there about that there's no evidence that – or there's nothing that supports that semen was on the skin of Janet Walsh here in this case. Do you remember that?"

Perlin: "I do."

Martocci: "Now, the autopsy that was performed in this case of course was performed back in 1979, right?"

Perlin: "Yes."

Martocci: "And there's a second part of this trial, I think, that you realize that there's no evidence that there was any semen on her skin because it just wasn't seen back at that time? You agree with that, right?"

Perlin: "It wasn't seen, but the question is whether it would be – would have been expected to have been seen."

Martocci: "But you can't say it wasn't there at all, right? You can't say that? That's what you told this jury, that you cannot say it with certainty, or with scientific certainty?"

Perlin: "I can say that it wasn't noted in anybody's report that it was seen."

But, Perlin noted, for something not to be seen doesn't mean it wasn't there.

"If someone is expecting, if someone is looking for an object, and they don't see an object, and their job is to report on what they see, and there's – and it's not reported, the same way that the report said, 'no traces of foreign evidence,' then that's information," he said. "That's negative information, but it's reported as not being seen."

Moving to an explanation of Perlin's TrueAllele system, Martocci asked the witness if the system could draw evidence from a DNA sample that human analysis might find inconclusive.

"That's correct," Perlin responded.

"And," countered Martocci, "TrueAllele removes any kind of human bias that might come into this? Is that right?"

Perlin: "In the sense that when it solves the problem, it has no access to the reference samples to be compared with. It has – it doesn't – it can't get an answer that you might be looking for. We have – often have very disappointed prosecutors."

The two men then moved to a scientific discussion of false positives that could occur in DNA sampling.

A false positive, Perlin explained, might occur when the probability of a genotype produced from a DNA test reveals a match statistic in a random population that is a low number, which would be below a zero threshold. In this exclusionary process, Perlin's TrueAllele system "generates hundreds of thousands of alternative hypotheses, alternative theories or explanation of how it can account for the peak data that it's seeing at every one of those … locations and then determines which explanations are more probable, which are less probable, and then it reports, those results," Perlin explained.

So, Martocci said, "that explanation of what is probable and what is less probable is the ultimate purpose of going through your computer system to answer the question toward, 'does the suspect match the evidence and a random person,' and the ultimate question is answered after the match comparisons?"

"Yes," Perlin replied. "At the source level, that's exactly the question that's being answered."

And, Martocci asked, in his system's comparison of seminal stains, "you developed negative numbers and positive numbers, and those positive numbers you would consider to be what you call inclusion? Is that safe to say? Any positive information you considered inclusion?"

"No," Perlin responded. "I would say that it is a suspected inclusion." If the number is a quadrillion, he testified, "that's an inclusion. If the number is ten or fifteen, then that's more likely than not, but that's not an inclusion."

Thus, Martocci suggested, "the higher the negative number would be stronger evidence of exclusion? Is that safe to say?"

Perlin answered in the affirmative.

At this point, Martocci put on display some tables showing sets of numbers attributed to the various evidence samples already discussed during the trial. He and the witness agreed that the numbers for Hopkins were higher than for Scott Walsh on the sheet – but Walsh did register as a positive as opposed to a negative.

Similarly, Hopkins' numbers for the night-gown were high – 15.

"That means that the match between Mr. Hopkins and the nightgown top is about a qua-drillion times more probable than a random person having contributed their DNA, random actually," Perlin explained.

Further defining the meaning of this num-bering system, Martocci moved to the blue robe's numbers for Janet Walsh.

"The eight is definite. The five is pretty def-inite. The two, probably" for Janet Walsh, Perlin explained in reference to the numbers for different spots on the robe.

Enter into evidence now the robe cord used to bind the victim's hands.

But first, Martocci introduced the notion that Perlin's method might not be completely scientific because the defense expert had subjectively classified the cord as evidence to be considered as part of the "clothing category" as opposed to the "death category," even though it played an instrumental role in her death because it bound her hands, making her struggle against her assailant more difficult. He could have put the cord in both categories, Martocci reasoned.

"Yes," Perlin said.

"Which you didn't do, did you?" Martocci asked.

"I don't think it would have made any difference to the facts that were being presented," Perlin answered.

Martocci: "Well, it seemed to make – it seemed to make a difference, doctor, because what we have in the one death chart, your death chart, was the handkerchief, which that would be obvious. That's the ligature that caused the strangulation, right?"

Perlin: "Uh-huh."

Martocci: "Okay. And you included the fingernails, right?"

Perlin: "Correct. Those are …"

Martocci: "Now, you associated fingernail scrapings with DNA that could be found in death, with death, because the person could have struggled and have, um, their assailant's DNA underneath their fingernails. Is that safe to say?"

Perlin: "True."

Martocci: "And you deliberately put that there because you thought that that should be so, using your human classification, not your computer, and you put that in there in your death paper?"

Perlin: "Yes. I've done – I've handled cases where these sort of items of evidence were involved in death."

So, Martocci suggested, her hands being bound removed "any opportunity to scratch anybody because of the bathrobe cord that you left out of the chart? Is that right?"

Perlin: "In the summary, the way I wrote

it, I – I classified items …"

Martocci: "But you were paid by the defense to be here today to get him as far away as you could from the DNA evidence, and part of that in your report is that you left him out of the chart that deals directly with death? According to your view of classification, you left him out of that and associated it just with clothing? When you did your report, it is what it is?"

Perlin: "I was paid minimally by the defense to give the most objective view that I could of this case …"

Martocci: "But it wasn't an objective view, based on what you said."

Because the prosecution hypothesis considered no alternative for how the death occurred, Perlin explained, "it was incumbent on someone – usually it's the prosecution to have that be done in this case – to bring, to offer some alternative hypothesis."

If it would please Martocci to move the cord to a different category, Perlin said, "we can mark it, move it, if that makes you happy, but the truth is, science demands that you must consider alternatives. You can't just say, 'I have one explanation; that must be it.' That's not science. That's somebody's opinion unbalanced by alternative explanations."

What he was asking, Martocci said, "is that you made a decision to not place that cord on that chart, and now you are saying that scientifically, you would question them both? That's all I am asking you."

"I am saying," Perlin replied, "you could put it in both, yes."

Martocci: "All right. But you didn't in this case? Is that fair?"

Perlin: "That's true."

Having established subjectivity in the assignment of category for the cord, Martocci moved to an exploration of the sweat theory. He asked Perlin to summarize the theory.

"The old stain that had been left prior," Perlin testified, "before the time of death through normal semen transfer, being a transfer, could have then transferred during the time of death, um, with – moisture and with pressure and in that way have provided a scenario where there's invisible semen left at two locations that were near each other."

That also is how the semen got on the robe, he testified – transferred through a layer of perspiration on Janet Walsh's skin, "two different cloth or fabric materials that are in the same location don't need to be explained by some direct ejaculation at a particular time. It's a viable alternative."

Martocci asked for the clothing chart to be displayed again and asked Perlin if he saw anyone else's DNA on the nightgown top or the bathrobe cord, "other than the defendant?"

"No," Perlin replied, "but in forensics, the absence – absence of evidence isn't evidence of absence."

Returning to the chart, Martocci then led Perlin through a list of suspects and their corresponding numbers for the various evidence items. Robert McGrail, for example, was associated with negative numbers, or numbers of exclusion entirely.

"Yes," Perlin confirmed. "That's what I said relative to these eighteen items."

The chart offered similar results for the unknown depositor of DNA on the bathrobe – which had produced the only positive number for the unknown person.

Scott Walsh, as noted previously, was associated with a positive number – albeit a low-density one – for one spot on the flat sheet, but the rest of his numbers were exclusionary.

Martocci moved the questioning to the handkerchief used to strangle Janet Walsh – "the best piece of evidence that you would draw any kind of DNA from, DNA that would help us match the killer? Would you agree with that?"

"That's true," Perlin answered.

Martocci: "And according to your chart that you did, that you don't have any – anybody on there?"

Perlin: "That's correct."

Having established that the bandana was the best location for finding a DNA match to the killer, along with planting in the jurors' minds the notion that Perlin had subjectively placed certain items of evidence in the wrong analytical category, Martocci pounced.

Perlin's computer analysis, he noted, had found positive DNA numbers for Hopkins on the ligature knot, where the state's DNA lab had, "found an uninterpretable DNA profile from the knot of the ligature, your system took that information and found positive numbers that you showed on your match sheet which you did not present to the jury, right? Is that not correct?"

Perlin: "That is not correct. This system …"

Martocci: "This is the …"

Perlin: "Can I object?"

The court: "He's – he's asking the questions. You are answering them. You will be able to explain your answer, but let him ask the question."

Martocci asked Perlin to explain.

"When you have a system – as I said before, you have – you have a distribution," Perlin testified. "When you have a bunch of positive numbers, like two, two and a half, three, two and a half, two point seven, so on, you get a distribution of what those numbers are.

"It's an average, it's a value, and if there

are reproducible amounts of variation around a central number, then that number is then what you have in the report. Here, you read, there was a number of small negative numbers, small positive numbers, and the negative numbers and the positive numbers fall in a distribution. The average data that you get from that is strictly that the average around point three might correspond to the matches, and you are seeing then a variation.

"Now, as a prosecutor, you look at a set of positive numbers and negative numbers, and you choose to only talk about the positive numbers and not talk about the negative numbers. Fortunately, that's not what we do.

"We looked at distribution, and we looked at everything that was found, and we averaged it, and in this case, that number did not reach one, so that's statistically bad, and we would never write that down."

Martocci reminded Perlin of his previous testimony and the notion that the amount of DNA "does matter."

"However," Martocci asked, "you did state in your testimony earlier, you said that that is a positive association even though it's close to zero? If it's above zero, it's a positive association, and everyone else on this spreadsheet is excluded. Isn't that correct? The only positive numbers are associated with the defendant, himself, in the knot from the ligature? Is that not right?"

The number relating to Hopkins on the knot, Perlin said, was "inconclusive. It's a – it's grantedly variable around zero, but you don't report it."

And yet, Martocci countered, Perlin's chart did report Scott Walsh's DNA on the flat sheet, which was, "you said, close to a one … but you put it on your chart or your report, didn't you?"

"Because it was low," Perlin replied.

"Right," responded Martocci, "But you – but you still put it in – on that chart, the bed sheets as was stated in this courtroom by the defense, that that is something that the Pennsylvania State Police, excuse me, couldn't find, but you found it, and that's a DNA match to Scott Walsh, so you are saying that for the defense, there are no matches? Is that accurate?"

Perlin: "I don't know."

So no one, Martocci argued, "no one else is even close to being inclusive, at least to the knot, except for the defendant?"

Perlin: "So I agree with you. The evidence can be …"

Martocci: "That's not what I'm asking."

Perlin: "But evidence can be inconclusive, and in this case, the way you followed it, this is inconclusive, so it's true: Evidence can tell you nothing."

"So the best you can say, Dr. Perlin," parried Martocci, "is that with regard to the ligature-bandana-handkerchief that you put on the chart that associates with – associates with death, you can exclude everyone else but the defendant himself?"

"No," responded Perlin. "I can say it's an interesting statement, but the statement that was made in the number is that it's not informative."

Martocci: "But it was also not excluding? It isn't a negative number, and it is certainly not any evidence that you made an exclusion based on the higher negative numbers that we saw on the evidence sheet? Isn't that right?"

Perlin: "I wouldn't interpret it that way. I'm sure you could have other people use that language."

***

Actually, Martocci would use that language himself in his summation to the jury – the next and final stage of this trial. Martocci, having used the defense's strongest DNA evidence – a positive finding for Hopkins' DNA not only on the nightgown, cord tie and flat sheet, but also now on the ligature knot – against Hopkins, would invoke science and character to depict the defendant as a womanizing murderer finally brought to justice by a bit of saliva on a cup.

Ross would do his best to argue for acquittal based on science and flawed investigation, suggesting to the jury the possibility of other perpetrators and highly selective and tainted evidence.

11

Defense attorney James Ross began his closing argument with a quote from his star scientific witness, Dr. Mark Perlin, that while physical evidence may ring true, " 'only in the interpretation of that evidence can there be error,' and that's what this case is about."

Ross thus invoked for the jury the concept, the theme of his defense, that science and evidence offer facts and data, but the human element of how those facts and data are analyzed, observed and understood played a significant role in this case – from the possibility of DNA evidence degraded or tainted, to selective analysis of that evidence that could have excluded other potential perpetrators.

Perlin, Ross argued, testified that he had never seen a case "in which the alternatives were not considered" – alternatives in this case raised by fluoresced staining found by an alternate light source on the items of evidence that never was tested because the state lab analysts had only looked at DNA deposited by sperm. Thus, in their scientific method, they had ruled out the possibility of anybody other than Hopkins committing this murder. Beyond that, though, Ross asked the jurors to consider how the police investigation of the case had been handled – which, in his opinion, was badly. Back when the clothing and other items of evidence were first analyzed in September of 1979, he said, "every one of these items, ladies and gentlemen, were completely clean of any observable trace evidence, and I ask you: does that make sense?"

And in later analysis, after DNA forensics had developed, a young female technician with just over two years of experience "created a travesty," Ross argued. "She looked at sixty-six areas of the nightshirt, on the robe tie, and on the sheets. What did she tell you she did? She looked at areas for evidence of sperm. Just 18.2 percent. Fifty-four fluoresced that were not sperm. That's 81.8 percent of the evidence that she disregarded."

There was no attempt by these lab technicians, Ross said, to ask about the possibility of sperm on the victim's wrists or hands in a case that the investigators and prosecutors had decided, once the spermal evidence was found through DNA analysis after 2010, had a sexual element and thus discarded all non-spermal evidence. The lab technician, Ashlee Mangan, "made a decision in a vacuum," Ross argued. "She decided, as she said, that 'sperm profiles were the easiest to detect, so that's what I'm going to do.' "

Displaying a document on the screen, Ross asked the jury to "look at all of the areas that fluoresced in which there is no sperm identified, and I asked Miss Mangan, 'what did you do? Did you disregard these?'

" 'Yes, I did.'

" 'Why?'

" 'Well, sperm was easier to detect.'

"Ladies and gentlemen, does that make sense?"

The prosecution, Ross argued, did not even know that the non-spermal fluoresced areas of the evidence had been ignored.

"They never even went back and checked those, and I'll tell you what: They didn't even know that this is what she did. They didn't find out until we were in this courtroom."

Once the investigators found Hopkins' DNA on the clothing and other items, Ross asked, "isn't it incumbent upon you to go back and test these other items and see if his DNA would also show itself in other areas, on the clothes she had on that night, like other areas to test for non sperm?

"No. They had their man, ladies and gentlemen. They were focused on their man. That was it, and it was easy. Sperm was the easiest thing to find."

Ross turned the jurors' attention to the bathrobe found at the crime scene. After Hopkins had been charged, the investigators then asked Mangan to test it.

"Over forty-six areas fluoresced but she didn't test all forty-six."

Sperm was found on the robe, Ross argued, "but you remember the email that led up to that?

"For an example, the bathrobe, because the tie obviously came from that bathrobe, and if there's no sperm on the bathrobe, then that means that Mr. Hopkins took the robe tie off the robe and tied up this woman's hands, and that would clearly prove that he was there that night, but also, if his sperm is on the bathrobe, then that means he wiped himself with the bathrobe, so if it's not there, he's guilty. If it's there, he's guilty.

"Does that make sense?

"Is that a theory – is that a theory that convinces you beyond a reasonable doubt?"

And the sperm they found, he said, was of an unknown person.

"Never once did they go back and check it."

The police, Ross argued, had no other evidence of Hopkins' presence at the crime scene.

"No one sees his car on the street. There's no evidence that my client had known that she was out that night.

"All they have is his sperm, his sperm that should have been there, the sperm that I told you was there, the sperm that they didn't even test, the sperm that our expert told you he found that wasn't the defendant's, no other evidence found.

"This huge and crazy investigation, ladies and gentlemen, leads to the arrest of Mr. Hopkins, but it does something else. It serves to make some other suspects that you heard about, because, if you remember, and we'll talk about this in just a minute, all of these other people were suspects because of all the things that they knew about, and so forth. They were eliminated simply because their DNA was not there. Think about that. The only DNA they tested was sperm.

"If you have these other people there, and if perhaps this was not a sexual act or any prelude to a sexual act that never occurred here, don't you think you should check to see if those persons' DNA were there, that you might find them, epithelial cells, anything, before you eliminate them?

"Did they do that? No."

Ross turned his attention to other suspects.

"Robert McGrail was at the disco bar the night before, dancing with Janet Walsh, hitting on her afterwards at Perkins, then stumbling home over a dark hill at 4 a.m., and he'd lost his checkbook, which was found half a block from Janet Walsh's house days later.

"You saw his demeanor on that stand. Could he look at you? No.

"This man was eliminated simply because his sperm was not found in these areas."

Scott Walsh, the victim's estranged husband, was involved in a sexual tryst with his girlfriend at 2 or 3 in the morning the day of Janet's murder and was home at 4 a.m. when his neighbor Margie Farinacci, who he knew was out with Janet that night, arrived home – at about the same time he is getting a phone call from the high school girl with whom he had just seen in his home an hour before. So he is awake at that time. And Walsh had admitted to following Scott Hopkins after first denying it – "this man was deceptive on five interviews," Ross argued.

Despite their strong suspicions regarding McGrail and Scott Walsh before the DNA evidence came along, Ross argued, the investigators and prosecuting attorneys dismissed their feelings – legitimate ones, considering their testimony and demeanor, Ross suggested – about these two suspects once the DNA match to Hopkins was obtained. Why? "Because they had another fish to fry," he said. "That's why."

As for the science in the case, Ross argued that Dr. Cyril Wecht's testimony was weak.

"The best that he could say was that Mr. Hopkins' semen was likely deposited at or around the time of the incident," Ross said of Wecht's testimony. "What does that mean? Does it mean the day before, a week before, two weeks before, a month before?

"He said it was unlikely that it was deposited on other occasions, and this from a man who asked Dr. Perlin to write the DNA chapter in his forensic science book," Ross argued, offering his own ace witness as the true expert in this case. "So who knows more about DNA? Dr. Wecht or Dr. Perlin?"

On that point of expertise, Ross cited Wecht's testimony to buttress his argument regarding selectivity of analysis. Wecht had said, Ross reminded the jury, "that it was a mistake not to analyze all of the fluoresced images. It was a mistake not to do that, to consider the clothes that were on the ironing board, this coming from the prosecution's own witness.

"He criticized their own case. He said that, right, but I ask you to compare and contrast that testimony of Dr. Wecht with the defense expert's, and I want you to think about this."

In an attempt to cast further doubt on Wecht's testimony, concerning the dispersion of sperm on the victim's body, Ross asked why there was no sperm found on her hands, wrists or fingers.

"Why isn't it on her body?

"If this man, my client, according to Dr. Wecht, is in this wild rage and strangling and spewing sperm, where is it?

"Why is it invisible?"

Also, how does anybody know that Janet Walsh was not on her knees, "and if that happens, the theory is gone."

As for the sperm that was found, Ross repeated, "it should be there. It was expected," because Janet Walsh had been involved with him sexually.

But, he summarized, "they want to ignore Dr. Perlin's report that he found someone to nine – I'm sorry – billion on the robe, and they wouldn't check that, but now we are going to use his findings on the knot that there was a zero chance there that that's positive.

"Ladies and gentlemen, that's what they had to rely upon. It's a sad state of affairs.

"The Pennsylvania State Police Crime Lab had wrote a report in 2005 and said that there's nothing on the handkerchief and another one in January of 2010, and they checked it twice.

"What they want you to do is engage in selective, selective believability."

Ross suggested that science supported the theory that the DNA could have transferred to the areas where it was found through the sweat that Janet Walsh produced while being strangled.

"Dr. Perlin told you that from a scientific standpoint, that is fortuitous findings. I want you to think about that."

As for the veracity of his other witnesses, Ross argued for the credibility of Hopkins' alibi.

"Larry Musgrave, does he strike you as a common man in Beaver County, working for Verizon, and his wife is a retired bank teller in Beaver County? Do they seem like someone you could count on? Do they have a motive to lie?

"Ladies and gentlemen," he continued, "they spoke to Mr. Musgrave four or five times, and they spoke to Georgeann twice, and you have heard about meeting at their house on January 29, 2012, and what the police said to them. Did anybody refute that? Did any police get up there and say that's not the way it was?

"He wants you to change your story, but Larry Musgrave didn't.

"You can't change the truth. You can't change the truth, ladies and gentlemen."

And Dianne St. George, he argued, confirmed the Musgraves' story.

"All they want you to believe is that Mr. Hopkins somehow stole out of that house, and does that make sense?"

And what of Hopkins, Ross asked. "What was his motive? Did they present any evidence of that?

"Why would a man kill a woman who was giving him free sex, and no one else knew about it? Why? Does that make sense? Is that something that you can rely upon?"

Hopkins had no opportunity, Ross argued.

"The clear evidence is that Janet Walsh returned home at 4 o'clock a.m., and the death occurred at 5 a.m., when Gregory Scott Hopkins was preparing for a pig roast the next day at that time.

"There were no cell phones. There were no computers or text messages."

Ask yourselves, Ross implored the jurors, "how he gets out of the house sometime after four, goes out to that residence, and is back there by five- thirty. There is no evidence."

Ask prosecuting attorney Frank Martocci, Ross urged, "what else you have besides the DNA."

His client is "no saint" Ross conceded. "He told you that he was a womanizer.

"Does that make him a killer?"

***

The response of prosecuting attorney Martocci would be that womanizing does not equal murder, but crime-scene DNA matched to Hopkins along with other testimony and evidence does.

While the defense had accused the prosecution of ignoring vital evidence, Martocci argued, that accusation was a diversion intended to take the jurors' focus toward evidence that was not there and away from the compelling evidence that was.

"What we do, as prosecutors, as the commonwealth, we follow where the evidence is, and that leads us to the conclusions that we make," he asserted. "That's how this works, so when the evidence is against you, like in this case, it's against them as strong as it is, what do you do? Pointing at you to not look at, pointing at you to look at all of these other things, pointing at you to say, 'well, maybe you should have looked at Robert McGrail, or you should have looked at Scott Walsh' – all of that," Martocci argued, was intended to divert the jurors from the truth "that he did it. It doesn't get much firmer in this case."

The prosecution may not have had fingerprints from the window of the victim's car, Martocci reasoned, "but we've got DNA." He continued: "We have DNA on – I'm going to say this a few times – the murder weapon. We have DNA on the murder weapon, and what is the murder weapon in this case? Remember that the murder weapon in this is the combination of the rope that had been on her hands and the bandana around her neck.

"That's the proof. It isn't just the DNA."

Photographs showed how Janet Walsh's body was positioned with a sheet deliberately pulled up over her top. The state had items of clothing, bedding, bandana and tie cord, all of which were sealed and stored separately "from day one." Of course when those items were first looked at in 1979 nothing was found then from visible examination other than blood and hair matches to the victim, "but that's all they could do then."

The DNA, Martocci observed, "didn't expire," but when the technology came along three decades later enabling another look at all the suspects, the investigators went where the evidence led them – to Hopkins, not because the investigating police decided to go after him. The evidence led to the defendant, he argued, "not because we decided we were going to do that.

"The evidence is there.

"That's what an investigation does. It goes through the evidence, and you look to everyone, and you start to eliminate."

In fact, he said, the investigators did look at alternate theories and suspects, including Scott Walsh and Robert McGrail.

"How this investigation works, is that you look at these other people and then eliminate them, and then the evidence takes you to the next thing and then the next thing, and what the evidence takes you to is him."

The reason the investigators and DNA technicians concentrated on the seminal stains, he explained, is because "this case has a sexual angle to it. When you look at the pictures, we all know that. That's obvious. Use your common sense.

"Janet Walsh is found deceased in her bed, naked from the waist down, only with a nightgown top on, so what is the best evidence source that you are going to have to identify who killed her?

"It's semen. That's it."

And the findings of semen on the nightgown and elsewhere were strong.

"The laboratory has four grades. Four-plus means that that is the most concentrated sperm density that you are going to have in simple terms, and that's important, that is an extremely important fact that led to the idea of Gregory Scott Hopkins' involvement."

At the time of Janet's murder, Martocci argued, Hopkins "ejaculated on her back, and that's how we got the seminal stain, and that sheet that he put on top of her afterwards – it was on top of the bed and the nightgown – that wet seminal stain transferred to the bed sheet. The only way to maintain that four-plus rating for the transfer from back of her nightgown to that flat sheet is that it would have to have been wet, and you know what Dr. Perlin said? The easiest transference is from a wet surface. That's where you get the same grade, the same grade."

Robert McGrail and the lost-and-then-found checkbook?

"No evidence of his DNA is on the nightgown."

If McGrail were sitting in the defense chair, Martocci asked, "what would you say? What would you think? That's why he's not there. Robert McGrail, Mr. Ross, would get over here and be screaming about all of the DNA that's not on that scene.

"He would be screaming about all of the DNA that's all over the deceased.

"He would be screaming about the DNA that's on that murder weapon and on the robe, so again, the evidence takes us to where we need to be."

Scott Walsh?

His DNA is not there either. His story, like McGrail's, has been consistent through the years; he expressed sorrow over the loss of Janet Walsh.

"Has the defendant?"

As for Scott Walsh's seminal DNA being

on the sheet of the bed, "if you follow Dr. Perlin's logic all the way through, that would be consistent with him being with her, because that was the marital bed. Those were the sheets from the marital house, and his DNA would have still been on it from that time.

"No," Martocci argued, the evidence "takes us to him" – Hopkins, because "as a cup is thrown where he sometimes gets a drink down at the Bridgewater Borough building, the defendant throws it away, and they get the evidence."

Again, the DNA is there.

The defense chose to put Hopkins, and thus his character, on the stand, Martocci argued.

That decision backfired.

"When that happens, you expose yourself to having your character attacked, and what we heard from the stand throughout the evidence, I will put it to you ladies and gentlemen, shows he's not to be believed at all about any of this. Just on the fact of the way he testified, I want you to consider, too, because when a person is lying to you about a very serious topic, what happens? You talk around it. That's what people do. You talk around."

The pig roast, the events of the evening before the murder, the character witnesses, Hopkins' construction business and the good work – including serving on the borough council – all had nothing to do with what he was on the stand for, Martocci argued.

"He decided to take the stand to convince you to believe him that he's not involved with this, yet he chose to talk about all the little things, about building all these houses and the septic tank.

"Did you really want to know all of that?
"No."

More important, though, was the pattern of lying established during the early stage of the investigation, when Hopkins lied about whether he knew Janet Walsh and, then, how well and how often he knew her, including in the Biblical sense.

"Finally, he says that he had sexual relations with her and that those sexual relations were just that, nothing else, just sex.

"She meant nothing, nothing to him, and

that was clear from his actions that day, where after finding out, what he initially said, which was, 'I don't know' that morning, 'that she was dead,' because the only person who would know that that morning would be the one that had killed her. Then he changed it later to, 'I found out,' or 'I knew from Joe Farinacci that – Farinacci that she was dead.'

"He never expressed any kind of sorrow over her loss," Martocci argued following a summation of Hopkins' lack of discussion with others about Janet's death, "not even when he testified, never.

"What does that say, that this is a little idea or a little snapshot into his character, into his soul?

"What did he say when I asked him, when he would go down to Janet's house for these secret get-togethers, for the secret relationship, 'you had sex with her until you ejaculated?'

"He said, 'until I was done.' Does this sound like a caring, honest, trustworthy person?

"Is that somebody who cared in the least about Janet Walsh?

"Does that give you a picture into his conscience, into his soul?

"It sure does."

The defendant, Martocci argued, "had even admitted to living a 'life of dishonesty.'

"He said that for the last thirty some years, he had built a way of getting from one relationship to another just by lying, and again, this is not about relationships.

"It's the lie, because when you go about lying as a second nature, and that's what he's done for thirty-four years, he told you, the problem is, when you are done, so for thirty-four years, since September 1, 1979, we know that that was easy for him, that that constant life-long deceit is second nature, so you have to consider that when you weigh credibility."

Martocci asked the jurors to ponder whether Hopkins' alibi witnesses could account for him "at the precise time the murder took place," as the judge would instruct them to consider. Martocci suggested to the jurors that Hopkins easily could have been up during the early morning hours, telephoned Janet, "shows up at her house then, and comes back.

"Impossible? Is that something that could have happened?

"Larry Musgrave told you it's not impossible. It's impracticable – that was his word – so can you account for him from 1:30 until 6 o'clock in the morning, when they say they started the pig roast?

"None of them can.

"Not one of those three people can account for his whereabouts from 1, 1:30 to 5:30, 6, not a single one of them."

All of them were asleep when Hopkins returned to the model home, Martocci argued.

And when they all got out of bed the next morning, "he's up. That's what they testified to. He's out there, preparing the pig roast."

And just how credible are these witnesses?

Larry Musgrave and his wife each wrote the same account of preparing for the pig roast that Friday night of the 1979 Labor Day weekend, in which they made the same mistake of suggesting that the pig had been turned by Hopkins and

Musgrave during the night, and then they amended their statement in 2010 "because now they realized that what they said back then doesn't make sense, so what do they do?

"Well, they rewrote it.

"Now, based on all of that, is that a solid alibi?"

Martocci then painted a long, verbal picture of what he conjectured happened that morning of Janet Walsh's death. According to this scenario: Hopkins gets out of bed early in the morning, phones Janet, goes to her home between 3:30 and 4 a.m., parks in the alley as he had always done, and goes into her apartment through her back door at her invitation. She is wearing the robe, which is found in front of her bed, takes it off when they enter the bedroom, and Hopkins grabs the cord from the robe.

"Now, at first, there may be some adventurous sex, not traditional, some bondage. It certainly appears to be, because he had to tie that rope around her before she died, based on the evidence.

"So he ties the knot, and you saw the knot.

Is it just nice and loose and easy to get out of?

"It's intricate. It's tight around her wrists, and again, it's what he did to her not to leave the bed.

"Okay. What does he do? How long does he tie her up once he was engaged in this asphyxia?

"Okay. It's part of the sex, so what does he do? He puts that bandana around her neck.

"That bandana around her neck is tight, that rope around her wrists is tight, and then he gets on top of her and starts to strangle her. What does he do?

"He ejaculates on her. We know that because of where his semen ends up, and then he starts to pull back on that – on that handkerchief."

Hopkins is the one perspiring, Martocci suggests, "on his hands, and his hands are holding that knot, so what does he do?

"He starts that process, starts the process of strangulation. That strangulation process lasts for how long? For ten to thirty second versus three or four minutes, it goes on from there, and that act of doing that, that's what leads us to the crimes that you have to choose from to find him guilty here in this case.

"That is, you will be told by the judge about the crimes that we have touched upon today that this defendant is facing. Those charges are involuntary manslaughter, voluntary manslaughter, third-degree murder, and first-degree murder, and I'm telling you that voluntary manslaughter and involuntary manslaughter I believe fail to fit this crime."

The crime, Martocci suggested, was either third-degree murder – death caused with malice – or first-degree murder – done with specific intent to kill and to do so with malice.

Finally, Martocci took the jurors back to the science and what he considered to be the most convincing piece of science in this case – the finding, thanks to Perlin's computer-generated analysis, of Hopkins' DNA, albeit a small amount, on the knot of the ligature.

"All of these columns here, there is not a single positive number that relates to that knot, not a single one," said Martocci, indicating a projected chart and the names of the other suspects, "and that means that all of these people on this row were all eliminated by the DNA evidence as to that ligature, as to the knot on her neck as being the murderer, except what do we have?

"We have positive numbers. This is Scott Hopkins from the top, all the way down.

"Those are all positive numbers, and those all correspond to particular pieces of evidence.

"The only person who cannot be excluded from that knot is the defendant," Martocci argued.

"You have to keep that in mind, that the only person of the people investigated here in this case, he's the only one."

Perlin, paid by the defense, Martocci argued, had tried to hide that information from the jury – evidence that "alone is proof beyond a reasonable doubt that he killed her, that, by itself."

The suggestion that Janet Walsh's sweat had caused a transfer of DNA from a previous sexual encounter, Martocci concluded, was "absurd. Just like Dr. Wecht said, we would have to believe in an absurdity."

After six hours of deliberation over two

days, the jury agreed, finding the 67-year-old Hopkins guilty of third-degree murder.

12

The verdict brought a decades-long sigh of relief to friends and family members who found closure to a case that had baffled the community and cops for more than 30 years. Janet Walsh's kid brother, Francesco Caltieri – he had changed his last name from Caltury back to the original spelling – expressed relief to a reporter for the Pittsburgh Post-Gazette in a story published on its front page November 23, 2013.

" 'You know, you hate to say joy, but I have to say joy,' " said the 53-year-old Caltieri, who had traveled from his Somerset, Ohio home to Beaver to testify and to witness the trial – which he said had been " 'painful' " due to the graphic photos and testimony about his sister's strangulation death.

The " 'horrible' " aspect of the ordeal, Caltieri said, was not knowing for so long who had killed Janet, and why.

" 'It's the first time that I think my sister's had the opportunity to feel peace and be at rest.

" 'She was what my mother called a "miracle baby," ' " Caltieri, the last surviving member of the family, told The Beaver County Times for a story published Sunday, November 24.

His sister had nearly died following a breach birth, he said, and was "sickly," according to the newspaper. "Consequently, she was home a lot with her brother. 'I can still see us like it was yesterday at the dinner table,' " he said.

" 'We just used to look out for each other,' " Caltieri said.

He remembered a time when he was in first grade and the teachers were lining up pupils for the bus and he couldn't see his big sister.

" 'I desperately wanted to find my sister to get me on the right bus home,' he said. He said he was fretting until he saw her, then 'I knew I'd be OK.' "

He told the newspaper that it was difficult hearing Janet's reputation " 'thrown under the bus,' but he was determined to be there for the entire trial.

" 'I wasn't able to be there that night to fight for her. By God, I was going to be here, on my knees if necessary, to fight for her now,' Caltieri said."

He described for the newspaper an active sister who played the oboe, participated in choir, was a cheerleader and enjoyed sewing. Janet, he said, could go "to the fabric store after school, pick out a pattern and fabric and sew a dress for herself to wear on a date that night with her high school sweetheart and future husband, Scott Walsh."

***

In his separate interview with the newspaper, Walsh said that he had not thought about whether others considered him responsible for Janet's death – he just wanted justice for her, he said. " 'My faith in the Lord just comforted me.' "

The couple still felt love for each other, he added.

" 'We were high school sweethearts. We went to three proms together.' "

It was tough all of those years, not knowing who had killed his former wife and living with the doubts surrounding his relationship with her, he recalled in a later interview after being asked for an explanation about the two failed polygraph tests.

"During all of these years, I have been told or read in the papers that I have passed it, failed it, and it was inconclusive," Walsh said, suggesting that his emotions then might have contributed to the test results.

"At the time of Janet's murder, I was a 23-year-old kid, wondering what happened, why it happened, and just totally confused. In questioning before the tests, they asked me if I felt responsible for her death. I responded by saying not directly but indirectly because I felt if we were not separated she would not have been with Hopkins. I felt like I let her down and did not protect her."

***

The scene in the courtroom described by The Beaver County Times following the rendering of the verdict was one of hugging and weeping.

"After the jury was excused, Walsh's family and friends wept and hugged one another while Hopkins' family cried and hugged him just before he was handcuffed and led away by a sheriff's deputy."

***

Andrew Gall, today the assistant chief of detectives for the Beaver County District Attorney's Office but then a rookie cop on the Monaca Police Department, was the one constant presence throughout this 34-year ordeal. He had stayed with the case from its inception and pushed it through to its conclusion. He told the newspaper this was the first time he'd ever cried in the courtroom.

" 'I always knew it was him,' " Gall told the newspaper. " 'I just wish it wouldn't have taken so long.' "

But until the DNA came along, there could be no certainty.

"The single most frustrating part" of the case, he said in a later interview, "was that I knew we had interviewed the killer but that none of us could decide which one it was. We could make arguments for each of the five suspects, and we all had a favorite. A good whodunit makes a good book or movie, but it is frustrating to live."

More thorough interviewing might have helped solve the case sooner, but police procedures were different then, Gall explained. During the initial interview process, "the more experienced investigators said that we should only talk to Larry Musgrave unless he gave us the impression he was clearly lying. It was procedure in 1979 to avoid talking to the wives/girlfriends so as not to ruin the marriage or relationship. If one of my detectives took that attitude now, he would be sent out immediately to correct his error."

Given the chance to do it over, Gall said, he would interview "all three alibi witnesses that Hopkins named. My gut reaction back during the initial interview was that he needed to be looked at harder. The more experienced investigators, who were all top-notch, read him differently and dismissed him early. I couldn't let him go and kept tabs on him over the years."

The other detectives were leaning toward Scott Walsh as the strongest suspect, especially after the results of the polygraph tests came in. But there is good reason that these results are not allowed into court, Gall said.

"Polygraphs are not admissible in court even today. I agree that they should not be. The value of a polygraph for me is to clear a suspect if you think he did not do it. They are also valuable for seeing if a suspect will agree to take one. This is always a good sign of innocence or arrogance, and then when they actually show up for the test – this is a great sign of innocence or arrogance. The polygraph operator is usually a skilled inter-viewer with a hammer – the box – hanging over the suspect's head."

Walsh's explanation regarding his state of mind during the polygraph exams meshed with Gall's.

"It should be noted that most polygraph

operators will tell you that Scott Walsh was given his first polygraph too soon after the incident. His emotions would be still too raw. Most operators will refuse to give a second polygraph to a person that was already tested. I think the fact that he voluntarily took two tests and agreed to be hypnotized and came every time – we estimated about a dozen interviews – I called him is much more telling of his innocence than failing those polygraphs tells of any guilt."

Hopkins, on the other hand, was a less willing participant in the process, and his demeanor and character heightened suspicion.

"Even though Hopkins had the best alibi of any of the suspects, you can't deny these facts," Gall said. "He tried to deny even knowing Janet Walsh in the initial interview, even after acknowledging knowing her – he tried to distance himself by time and said that it was only a sexual relationship. Hopkins was divorcing his first wife, romancing Dianne St. George who became his second wife, and was showing Polaroids of other girls that he was involved with to his workers on the job site. Women he was involved with at the time stated that he was very open sexually and willing to try new things. He was driving a Porsche and the business was a success at the time – before the steel industry collapsed and the bottom dropped out.

"He was the only suspect that refused to give DNA when asked," Gall continued. "The placement of the DNA on the rope, the nightgown and the sheet was paramount. He had been involved with her before but for his DNA to be in the locations it was in was the key. Even his expert, under cross-examination, said that Hopkins was the only suspect that could not be eliminated from the knot in the handkerchief."

So why, as Hopkins' defense attorney had asked the jury, would Hopkins kill a secret lover with whom he was enjoying free sex?

"I still don't have a theory on the how and why," Gall answered. "I am not sure if it was some sexual adventure that went terribly wrong or if he went there with the intent to kill her. He did not seem to have much respect for her as a person in any of the interviews I had with him. The ruling of murder three means the jury wasn't sure which one it was either. Deputy Coroner Harper Simpson felt that she did not die quickly. Only Hopkins can tell us for sure, and he is not talking."

***

Indeed, Hopkins refused a request, through his attorney, to be interviewed for this book.

So, we are left with conjecture and hypothesis – and with what Gall identified as one of the bigger ironies in this case. That is, while the jury believed that sex apparently gone bad was behind this murder, the jurors – particularly the female members of the panel, according to Gall – did not fall subject to his womanizing charms; his character, in fact, did him in.

"We thought this was strictly sex," one female juror said in a post-trial interview, "like he didn't care about the person, and that sets the profile that after all was said and done, he was done with her. He didn't try to revive her, didn't call the police, nothing. He proved that he was such a person that he would do that sort of thing, she meant nothing to him, and that's the biggest thing against him, like yes, he would definitely do something like that."

The biggest mistake the defense made in the trial, she said, was putting Hopkins on the stand – a ploy intended to demonstrate to the jurors that he wanted to tell them his story, a tactic intended to help him connect with the jurors. It had the opposite effect.

"Through his testimony, you could see the true man," this female juror said. "You could see that this person was not an honest person, the way he talked." It was clear, the juror said, that Janet Walsh "meant nothing" to Hopkins.

As for the defense expert, she said, he "obviously was a paid witness for the defense, and that is all that I took into consideration, he was doing a job that he was paid for, and he was trying to look for anything that could be on the negative side of the proof."

Similarly, Hopkins' alibi witnesses did not help his case.

"It seems like it would be easy to get out

of the house without anybody knowing about it," said a male juror during a post-trial interview.

Drinking was going on that Friday night, he said; "they'd had a party, and you know how that goes."

Like the female juror, this juror was surprised that the defense put Hopkins on the stand.

"What came out of his mouth, it backfired on them, I think."

One of Hopkins' statements shot down his spine, the juror said, "when he made a joke out of whether he had an orgasm with her. Really? You're fighting for your life here dude, and this is what you're going to say?"

Similarly, the testimony of the defense expert witness ended up hurting Hopkins more than helping him, said this juror.

"That was kind of the point, you know, point of the fact that he was trying to say, 'oh, there's hardly anything there, but the only thing we can find was his;' that was the telling tale – the only thing they could find was Hopkins. To us, it kind of proved that the only person that could have been on that knot was Hopkins. You turn

around, and the only evidence that pointed anywhere was Hopkins."

***

The other constant throughout this case,
besides Gall, was Janet Walsh's father, Peter Caltury, who, Gall said, "never lost faith in the police. He would call me or I would call him. He
never screamed or yelled or complained. He just
wanted to know that we had not forgotten the
case and his daughter. I assured him I would never stop looking. His wife became bitter over the
years, and she would call the state police. Mary
Jane would keep Trooper Frank Keenan on the
phone for a long time, revisiting every point of
the case."

Gall's wife, Tammy, was working as a
hairdresser at a care home and rehabilitation
center a few years after the murder, and one day
was working on a woman "who seemed somewhat stern and angry," Gall said. "The lady got
Tammy's last name. She asked if she was related
to me. The lady was Mary Jane Caltury, and she

told Tammy 'he OWES me!' and told her that her daughter had been murdered. Tam said 'if your daughter is Janet Walsh, he has not forgotten, I hear about the case all the time.' "

Which she did.

"Tammy heard me fret and moan about the case for years and remembers me going on my own time with Trooper Frank Keenan to follow things up before I went to the DA's office," Gall said. "Tam told me afterward how different Pete and Mary Jane were and felt that it all stemmed from Janet's death."

This case, Gall said, was one of his three most memorable ones.

***

"I arrested a woman for killing her twelve-year-old daughter who probably killed at least one or maybe both of her other daughters. She had them listed as SIDS (Sudden Infant Death Syndrome). It was a long and difficult investigation."

The other memorable case, he said, affected him personally.

"Tam was pregnant, and we lost the baby in the middle of December. On December 19, people at the recycling center found a newborn baby in the trash. The baby had been born alive and wrapped in clothes and thrown away. I was part of tracking down the mother and charging her. That one came at the wrong time for me and I wouldn't let it go."

The Janet Walsh case, though, "will be the one I bore my grandkids with someday," he said. "I simply felt good and as if I had just finally completed an arduous task. It was one of the most satisfying clicks of the handcuffs I have ever heard, and I have cuffed a large number of people over the years, from simple drunks to killers.

"My personal thing is that he didn't mean to murder her," Gall said as we sat in his car along the river bank down the road from Hopkins' house and watched the Beaver River empty into the Ohio. The houses of Upper Monaca, where Peter Caltury and his daughter and son-in-law lived, loomed above the river on the opposite bank.

"He went there for his latest kinky sex thing and this was an accident. It would have been a manslaughter type of thing if he would have come and told us so. In reality, this is 1979, if he would have called an ambulance and the police back then, nothing would have happened to him. If he would have called and said, 'look, we were having kinky sex here, something went wrong, she died,' he would have been charged with manslaughter, even involuntary manslaughter, and just been given probation.

"Y'know, he killed a guy in a traffic accident. He was involved in a traffic accident just out of high school, he died, and it was all fine. And he didn't have a whole lot of remorse about that either."

***

Three months after he was convicted of the murder, Hopkins was back in court, this time to learn how long he would spend behind bars. But first, he would hear the angry and sorrowful testimony of the remaining family members and friends of Janet Walsh – testimony that would summarize how murder in a small town can devastate family, friends, and community.

Francesco Caltieri told the court that the murder of his sister ruined his life, according to the February 27, 2014 account of the sentencing hearing by The Beaver County Times.

" 'I haven't been the same since,' " he said, telling of his paranoia following her death, not knowing who might be the killer. His brother, Joe, who died like his mother without knowing who killed his sister, "would burst into tears at the mention of their sister's name and cried himself to sleep for a long time after her death," reported the newspaper.

" 'My mother, shortly thereafter, became a zombie,' " Caltieri testified. " 'There were days and days on end where she wouldn't come out of the bedroom. She became a hollow shell.' "

Caltieri asked Judge Harry Knafelc to impose a 34-year sentence on Hopkins.

" 'Give him the same time incarcerated that he has caused myself and my family to be incarcerated,' he said."

Caltieri then looked at Hopkins.

" 'Mr. Hopkins, you took my sister's life. It was not yours to take,' Mr. Caltieri said. 'My religion tells me I'm supposed to pray for you. You're the one that needs it. I'm supposed to forgive you, but I'm not there yet.

" 'I wish for once in your life you would man up, tell us, for God sake, why,' " Caltieri told Hopkins. " 'I'm not praying for you anytime soon. You can go straight to hell.' "

Janet Walsh's former husband told the court that " 'there is not a day that goes by that I don't think about it.' "

He has " 'dealt with years of anxiety and depression,' " Walsh testified, adding that " 'the only person he (Hopkins) ever cared about was himself.' "

Janet Walsh's childhood friend, Susan Neiderdal, told the court that Janet had been " 'like my little sister.'

" 'It changed me, who I am as a person,' " the newspaper reported of her testimony. " 'The pain never goes away. The thought of how she was brutally murdered haunts me every day.' "

" 'You should never be allowed to be a part of society again,' " she said, facing Hopkins. " 'You're a monster.' "

The judge had a story of his own for the convicted murderer.

"Knafelc said he was a young defense attorney at the time of her murder," the newspaper reported, "and he remembers friends and family who moved away from Monaca because they were afraid to live there.

" 'Nothing can be more difficult for a family than to lose a child,' Knafelc said, adding that Walsh's death 'diminishes all of us.' "

He then sentenced Hopkins to eight to 16 years in prison.

" 'This is the first time I can say I believe my sister is resting in peace,' " Caltieri told the newspaper following the sentencing. " 'It's finally done. He's going to jail.' "

The movies playing that long weekend leading into the remainder of Hopkins' life included "The Lego Movie" and "Endless Love" at the Cinemark in Center Township, and "American Hustle" "About Last Night" and "Lone Survivor" at the RobinsonTownship Cinemark. That Friday night, live entertainment at the Palms Brazilian Steakhouse featured the Miller Fortune Girls. Talerico's Bar & Grill Backroom Restaurant in Ambridge was gearing up for a St. Patty's Day party with a live DJ, giveaways and green beer. The Long Branch Saloon in New Brighton was offering a DJ along with $2 well drinks and $1 mystery shots.

On television that night, viewers had a plethora of choices, thanks to the innovation of cable TV that had come along since that weekend of Janet Walsh's death long ago. The small-screen menu included "Grey's Anatomy," "IMPACT Wrestling," "The Waltons," "Wild West Alaska," "American Idol," "Law & Order: Special Victims Unit" and one that Hopkins might find especially intriguing if allowed to watch it, "Cold Case Files."

Afterthoughts

In October of 1998, staff members of a nursing home in Lawrence, Massachusetts welcomed the birth of a baby girl to a 24-year-old resident of the nursing home. Trouble was, nobody knew the identity of the father. This is because the mother of the baby girl had been comatose for more than three years. Nursing home staffers didn't even know she was pregnant until just days before the delivery.

"Under the circumstances, the pregnancy had to be the result of rape; yet the woman was uniquely unable to name her assailant," according to Time magazine's June 11, 1999 account of the rape and subsequent birth. "If she couldn't speak, however, the blood of her daughter could. Shortly after the baby's birth, the police drew a sample of the infant's blood, then took voluntary samples from male relatives of the woman as well as from nursing-home personnel and others who might have had access to her. Comparing the men's DNA with the baby's, they figured, could lead them to the rapist."

Indeed, the statistical likelihood of identifying the rapist, if his DNA was found, was high. DNA testing, reported Time, could "yield remarkably accurate results. If three of the ministrands match a suspect's, the likelihood is 2,000 to 1 that police have the right person. Nine matches boost the odds to 1 billion to 1. FBI sampling rules require no fewer than 13 matches.

"Its success as a crime-fighting tool is incredible," Christopher Asplen, director of a national DNA-study commission, told the magazine. The Lawrence, Massachusetts scenario might sound familiar to followers of "Law & Order: Special Victims Unit," or other, similar television dramas of violent crime. But unlike those programs, in which the perp is discovered by the cops and dealt with by the courts by the end of the hour, this crime was in search of a resolution. Time reported that the DNA dragnet had yet to yield an arrest in the Lawrence case, but "it has led to controversy. Over the past decade, as anybody who followed the O.J. Simpson trial can attest, DNA profiling has become almost as important a part of crime fighting as fingerprinting. But even as technology pushes forensic science forward, the Constitution has worried it back. The Fourth Amendment guarantees citizens protection from unreasonable searches and seizures, and although the Founding Fathers didn't contemplate strands of DNA when drafting the Bill of Rights, what search could be more invasive than an assay of our very genes?"

Such concerns were raised, the magazine reported, when the New York City commissioner of police in December of 1998 recommended submission of a routine DNA sample by anyone arrested for a crime. In England, where the process of DNA testing in criminal investigations originated and "where a genetic database has operated since 1995, suspects are routinely screened this way – more than 360,000 gene prints are online – though police do promise that such profiles will be scrubbed from the record if the person is cleared," according to the Time analysis.

"English officials investigating a crime in a small town sometimes perform mass screenings in which thousands of people are asked to surrender a mouth swab full of DNA. The law gives anyone the right to decline, but as residents of Lawrence, Massachusetts, are learning, no law can prevent the slit-eyed look police give a person who actually chooses to exercise that right."

A member of the board of directors of the American Civil Liberties Union observed to the magazine: "There is no such thing as a technology like this without an ideology of surveillance and control behind it."

***

As the November 1998 issue of Newsweek analysis of DNA forensics cited in chapter 4 of this book points out, despite the reliability of the DNA evidence, this investigative technique raises several ethical and legal questions and potential problems.

One is establishing and preserving the integrity of the samples – the hair, clothing, blood and semen and other evidence and materials containing or carrying the DNA.

"Rapists deposit semen; intruders may cut themselves and bleed; assailants, if there was a struggle, may leave behind blood, hair or skin scrapings," wrote the article's authors. "Post-O.J. (Simpson) cops have become very aware of crime-scene protocol. 'We train our people to look at DNA first, because it's the most fragile,' says T.K. Martin, a crime-scene specialist for the Illinois State Police. The biggest danger is cross contamination from other samples. Material is collected with disposable tweezers and cops change gloves each time they pick up a sample; at a complex scene, Martin says, an investigator might go through 100 pairs of gloves."

Another question is the legality of the method of gathering evidence, such as that used by a St. Petersburg, Florida cop who followed a man matching the description of a robber suspected in 15 robberies and a double rape.

"Police believed that Charles Peterson was the perpetrator, in part because of his markedly toes-out gait, but they couldn't link him to any of the crimes," according to a 2000 edition of the national City Journal. "Though the cops had DNA evidence from the rapes, Peterson refused to supply them with a DNA sample for comparison. So the police got a sample another way. Trailing Peterson in an unmarked car as he drove his motorcycle around town, an officer saw him lean over and spit while stopped at a traffic light. The officer quickly pulled over and scooped up the spit with a paper towel. Lab analysis showed that the DNA from Peterson's saliva matched that of the forensic evidence. Cops had all they needed to cook the Duck Robber's goose."

Sgt. Michael Puetz, the St. Petersburg officer who gathered the evidence, told Newsweek that he believed in the constitutionality of his investigative technique, saying the courts "have held that once you've put out your trash, you've waived your right to keep the contents private, and 'I don't see why the same won't hold true for saliva.' "

Nonetheless, privacy concerns accompany the increasing use of this forensic technique.

Databases such as CODIS open up the specter of massive privacy invasions and the potential for DNA profiling by the government and other organizations or agencies – no small worry, in light of recent revelations of National Security Agency monitoring of citizen emails and telephone calls.

"The genetic sequences stored in the (FBI's) database are almost all 'junk' DNA, which contains no information about the person's traits," Newsweek's reporters observed. "Even if outsiders could obtain the data – and elaborate security measures are supposed to prevent that – they couldn't use it to predict, say, whether a person might be susceptible to schizophrenia or Alzheimer's. But the original blood samples, containing the full complement of DNA, would still be on file with the states, and they would be of great interest to insurance companies or prospective employers. And suppose scientists identify a gene that predisposes people to violence. A burglar, say, who has that gene may be more likely to commit a violent crime later. But should he be treated any differently as a consequence? America's most basic rule is that you can't lock people up for things they didn't do, even things they just didn't do yet."

***

DNA dragnets, such as the one used in the Pitchfork case cited in chapter 4 of this book, in which 5,000 people were asked to submit to DNA testing – a scenario that has come to involve thousands of involuntary DNA dragnet participants thanks to CODIS – also spark privacy concerns.

Newsweek spotlighted such a potential civil-rights infringement in its summary of the case in Lawrence, "where a near-comatose young woman in a nursing home was raped earlier this year and recently gave birth to a baby girl. With no suspects, Essex County District Attorney Kevin Burke last week began seeking DNA samples from about 30 men on the nursing-home staff who had access to the woman's room. So far, 'everybody has been cooperative,' said Burke, but he adds that 'if they don't volunteer, we will be compelled to seek a warrant (for an involuntary sample) through a grand-jury procedure.' The state ACLU suggests it would go to court on behalf of any employee who chose not to cooperate. Search warrants 'can't be a fishing expedition,' says ACLU director John Roberts, 'because a person works there doesn't meet the standard of probable cause.' "

***

Members of the congressional Office of Technology Assessment (OTA) did have an idea of the controversies that lay ahead when they recommended in 1990 the establishment of national standards for DNA testing. The FBI and other law enforcement agencies went on to codify the standards through a national databank of DNA markers. By the decade's end, the establishment of the CODIS databank had led to identifying hundreds of suspects in felony cases. But, as the OTA had recognized, such searches carry a civil liberties cost.

While recognizing that widespread use of DNA testing "could be a significant weapon in fighting crime," the Associated Press reported

August 4, 1990, the OTA urged that "quality assurance mechanisms should proceed without delay."

Sixteen states had created or were considering "creating DNA files for known offenders." With the FBI at that time considering creating its own national DNA databank, the agency warned of the potential for abuse. But the OTA predicted that creating such a databank "will 'evoke several concerns about privacy,' " the Associated Press report continued.

" 'Because DNA is specific to an individual and so highly personal, some are reluctant to see any DNA test results become part of a de facto national database.' ... The report said that Congress could play a role in the development of DNA testing by establishing standards and funding laboratories or training for personnel. But the OTA said Congress also will have to consider whether to establish national computer databanks of DNA information and wrestle with the concerns about privacy and civil rights in collecting and storing DNA profiles."

Congress and the FBI did establish language along this line. According to information posted on the FBI's Laboratory Services website:

"No names or other personal identifiers of the offenders, arrestees, or detainees are stored using the CODIS software. Only the following information is stored and can be searched at the national level:

"(1) The DNA profile – the set of identification characteristics or numerical representation at each of the various loci analyzed;

"(2) The Agency Identifier of the agency submitting the DNA profile;

"(3) The Specimen Identification Number – generally a number assigned sequentially at the time of sample collection. This number does not correspond to the individual's social security number, criminal history identifier, or correctional facility identifier; and,

"(4) The DNA laboratory personnel associated with a DNA profile analysis."

Also: "The computer terminals/servers containing the CODIS software are located in physically secure space at a criminal justice agency. Access to these computers is limited to only those individuals authorized to use CODIS and approved by the FBI. Communications between participating federal, state and local laboratories that occur over a wide area network accessible to only criminal justice agencies approved by the FBI.

"Pursuant to federal law (the DNA Identification Act of 1994), DNA data is confidential. Access is restricted to criminal justice agencies for law enforcement identification purposes. Defendants are also permitted access to the samples and analyses performed in connection with their cases. If all personally identifiable information is removed, DNA profile information may be accessed by criminal justice agencies for a population statistics database, for identification research and protocol development purposes, or for quality control purposes. The unauthorized disclosure of DNA data in the National DNA database is subject to a criminal penalty not to exceed $250,000."

We'll leave it to constitutional and civil liberties specialists to parse those paragraphs and to answer such questions as how such access decisions are made, and by whom. But a safe assumption is that despite these safeguards – or perhaps because of the terminology associated with them – privacy apprehensions remain when it comes to such national and state DNA databanks.

The continued rapid expansion of DNA testing and analysis for criminal investigations spurred discussion not only in the national lay press, but also in the academic and research journals, in which scholars pursued a myriad of ethical and legal concerns.

An overview of DNA fingerprinting in the criminal justice system published in a 2006 issue of the journal DNA and Cell Biology also cited concern over privacy, listing it as the "primary" legal, ethical and social issue of this technology.

"DNA can provide insights into many aspects of a person and their families including susceptibility to particular genetic disorders, legitimacy of birth, and fertility," according to the article. "This increases the potential for genetic discrimination by government, society and others. Therefore, DNA typing should be carried out in a very sophisticated way, and should meet all the international standards and follow and abide all the ethical, legal, and social concerns involved with DNA typing."

The use of DNA databanks, observed the researcher, "also involves some ethical issues and requires a balance between human rights and justice. Retention of samples for long periods of time is also risky, since this provides considerable accessibility to private genetic information."

This article also raised a couple of concerns that would emerge in the Janet Walsh investigation and ensuing court case: the potential for contamination.

"DNA testing faces (the) important problem of impurities of the sample," observed this researcher. "Very often investigators are not properly trained for sample collection and encounter problems in identification and collection of proper DNA evidence from the scene of (the) crime. Contamination of the samples and using the correct sample proper labeling, etc., are a few important aspects, which should be taken into consideration."

Finally: "Risk of false or misleading results from DNA testing and chances of tampering with the evidence cannot be ignored. Strict confidentiality is required as far as identity of the sample is concerned, and each sample should be tested by more than one examiner to confirm the results. Irrespective of having all these limitations, DNA fingerprinting is a very reliable technique for identification if used efficiently and intelligently."

***

Writing in the journal Science & Public Policy in March of the next year, Simon A. Cole of the Department of Criminology, Law and Society at the University of California, Irvine, raised an entirely new potential problem that, while not applicable to the Walsh case, merits serious consideration by criminologists and legal scholars nonetheless: the potential for racial bias in the use of this technology. In light of the growing evidence of racial and ethnic bias in criminal arrests, investigations and sentencing, this issue cannot be ignored in any overview of the use of DNA testing and technology.

"Two general positions on this question

seem plausible," wrote Cole, arguing that while DNA technology carries the potential of leveling the racial and ethnic playing field in criminal investigations, it also poses risks. The first position, he wrote, "is that experience has shown good old-fashioned detective work to be so imbued with inequality – with unfairness to minorities and the poor – that victims of inequality would be better off with a shift towards forensic technology. To be sure, forensic technology can be abused and misinterpreted, but, nonetheless, it could be argued that it carries with it an objectivity that renders it less susceptible to abuse than traditional police investigative methods. In other words, is the culture of police investigation so imbued with discrimination that any influx of science, scientists, or scientific culture is likely to have an ameliorative effect? In this view, the disenfranchised can only benefit from the increased use of science in criminal investigation."

But, argued Cole, the use of this technology also strengthens the capabilities of those who would abuse the justice system.

"Putting more powerful tools in the hands

of a law-enforcement system that differentially targets minorities, the poor, and inner-city neighborhoods will only exacerbate existing inequalities," wrote Cole. "DNA profiling may more precisely identify the author of a particular crime, but it wields only slight influence over which crimes are investigated and none over which prosecutions are pursued more vigorously or who is sentenced more harshly."

Equally troublesome is that DNA dragnets – "suspicionless searches in which residents of a neighborhood are asked to 'volunteer' DNA samples – samples that are often then retained by law enforcement – may fall more heavily on minorities, the poor, and others with less confidence in their ability to resist state authority."

Similar concerns exist in the "scope" of DNA databases, observed Cole. Expansion of databases beyond their use for such serious crimes as rape and murder, argued Cole, potentially incorporates "entire neighborhoods and ethnic communities into the database," and places "more than four times as much of the African-American population as the Caucasian population in a national database."

Cole cited statistics of United Kingdom DNA databases.

"UK Home Office figures indicate that 37% of black men, 13% of Asian men, and 9% of white men had their DNA samples included in the national database.

"There is little question," wrote Cole, "that arrestee databases represent the least equitable solution to the scope problem. This position is shared by a wide range of libertarian bedfellows from both the left and the right."

The importance of such issues, wrote Cole, "stems from the fact that criminal defendants are overwhelmingly drawn from the ranks of those who otherwise tend to be victims of inequality in our society, minorities and the poor."

In other words, as with any other crime investigative technique, data pools can be tainted by attitudes and beliefs.

Cole also identified troubling aspects of the use of DNA profiling or fingerprinting in the realm of gender inequality, arguing that while the practice more effectively places perpetrators at crime scenes, "it provides little help in cases in which identity is not an issue – acquaintance rapes and assaults in which the disputed issue is consent, rather than identity. Moreover, the existence of DNA evidence may be expected to shift a certain portion of defenses from identity to consent for the precise reason that identity can no longer be credibly contested. Thus, DNA evidence may shift some cases towards defenses that are harder on victims."

A 2011 analysis of forensic genetics published by GeneWatch, a bulletin of the Committee for Responsible Genetics, cited some of the same concerns and issues, noting that "many of the same problems that routinely plague criminal justice systems are reflected in these practices, including racial disparities in arrests and convictions. For example, while African-Americans are only 12% of the U.S. population, their profiles constitute 40% of the Federal database (CODIS)."

The article, penned by Jeremy Gruber, president of the Council for Responsible Genetics, and published in the August/September issue, identified techniques – including one that would be used in the Janet Walsh investigation – that it categorized as going "well beyond the mere identification of a person and … providing law enforcement unprecedented access into the private lives of innocent persons by way of their own genetic data without a court order or individualized suspicion."

Such techniques include:

- DNA dragnets in which police take samples from the public;
- Familial searching (also cited by Cole), in which partial matches of DNA evidence and databank profiles provide a list of possible suspects from relatives;
- Building "probabilistic profiles (including but not limited to race)" of suspects from crime scene DNA evidence;
- Surreptitious collections and searches of DNA left on items such as cigarette butts and drinking vessels;
- Creation of local "offline" DNA databases;

- Dismissing minor offenses in exchange for voluntary participation in DNA databases.

"At the same time that the growth of forensic DNA databases is exploding, there has been little public discourse on the privacy and human rights concerns they raise," argued Gruber, "nor has there been any domestic or international effort to create standards reflecting such concerns including those international bodies that are promoting information sharing. ... An appropriate middle ground between the legitimate needs of law enforcement and a respect for individual rights is achievable."

***

Beyond privacy rights and the obvious potential and actual infringement of constitutional guarantees regarding privacy and civil liberties – including Fourth Amendment implications regarding unreasonable searches – a primary legal concern regarding DNA testing and analysis in criminal investigations and trials is the problem of contamination. This issue also played a large role in the Walsh murder trial.

Writing in the July 29, 2013 issue of the ABA Journal, the journal's senior writer, Debra Cassens Weiss, argued that DNA evidence "may seem rock solid, but in some cases it has pointed to the wrong suspect."

For evidence, Weiss cited the case of Lukis Anderson, a 26-year-old bay area man who had been charged in the November, 2012 robbery and murder of a San Jose, California man based on DNA found in the victim's fingernails. The DNA evidence was entered into a database, "producing a hit," wrote Weiss. But law enforcement officials learned that the charged man "was in the hospital on the night of the crime, where paramedics had taken him because of severe intoxication."

After the wrongly accused man had spent five months in jail, "prosecutors recognized that he could not have been the perpetrator," Weiss wrote. "Prosecutors now believe that (his) DNA may have been transferred to the victim by the paramedics' clothing or equipment. The theory is still under investigation."

Weiss took her information for this piece from an op-ed commentary published in the July 24, 2013 edition of The New York Times, in which University of California, Hastings, law professor Osagie Obasogie cited a case in Germany in which law enforcement officials conducted a DNA search seeking a serial killer linked to six murders.

"In 2009, police recognized that the DNA was from cotton swabs used in the investigations, which had been contaminated with the DNA of the factory worker who made them," Weiss summarized.

In his op-ed piece, Obasogie also had criticism for DNA databases, writing that a 2005 audit of Arizona's DNA database "showed that, out of some 65,000 profiles, nearly 150 pairs matched at a level typically considered high enough to identify and prosecute suspects. Yet these profiles were clearly from different people.

"There are also problems with the way DNA evidence is interpreted and presented to juries," wrote Obasogie. "In 2008, John Puckett — a California man in his 70s with a sexual assault record — was accused of a 1972 killing, after a trawl of the state database partially linked his DNA to crime scene evidence. As in the Anderson case, Mr. Puckett was identified and implicated primarily by this evidence. Jurors – told that there was only a one-in-1.1 million chance that this DNA match was pure coincidence – convicted him. He is now serving a life sentence.

"But that one-in-1.1 million figure is misleading, according to two different expert committees, one convened by the F.B.I., the other by the National Research Council," Obasogie's piece continues. "It reflects the chance of a coincidental match in relation to the size of the general population (assuming that the suspect is the only one examined and is not related to the real culprit). Instead of the general population, we should be looking at only the number of profiles in the DNA database. Taking the size of the database into account in Mr. Puckett's case (and, again, assuming the real culprit's profile is not in the database) would have led to a dramatic change in the estimate, to one in three.

"One juror was asked whether this figure

would have affected the jury's deliberations. 'Of course it would have changed things,' he told reporters. 'It would have changed a lot of things.' "

Concluded Obasogie: "But when the government gets into the business of warehousing millions of DNA profiles to seek 'cold hits' as the primary basis for prosecutions, much more oversight by and accountability to the public is warranted. For far too long, we have allowed the myth of DNA infallibility to chip away at our skepticism of government's prosecutorial power, undoubtedly leading to untold injustices."

***

A lengthy September 1, 2013 ABA Journal analysis of suspect DNA techniques and evidence further eroded that myth of infallibility. In that analysis, senior writer and former Palm Beach Review and Sarasota Tribune-Herald reporter Mark Hansen detailed numerous cases of DNA- related errors.

One of the most horrendous of these was the massive fraudulent tainting of DNA evidence by former West Virginia state police crime lab serologist Fred Zain, which was revealed in 1993. According to Hansen's analysis, the work of Zain, who died in 2002 while awaiting retrial on charges of fraud that had resulted in a hung jury in a previous trial, came to light following the exoneration – based on DNA evidence – of a convicted rapist Zain had identified as the culprit. The resulting investigation revealed that Zain had falsified "as many as 134 cases during a 10-year period," Hansen wrote in the journal. "In fact, Zain was found to have tainted so many trials with false and misleading testimony, the judge assigned to investigate his work concluded that everything Zain ever said and did should be deemed 'invalid, unreliable and inadmissible' as a matter of law."

But the Zain case was just one of several instances of DNA analysis abuses, errors or tainted evidence as summarized by Hansen's ABA Journal expose. Another was that of a prosecution expert who had worked as a chemist in the crime lab of the Oklahoma Police Department and had testified in 23 death penalty cases in Oklahoma who was fired in 2001 for "doing sloppy work and giving false or misleading testimony."

More recently, the crime laboratory in St. Paul, Minnesota's police department in 2011 suspended drug analysis and fingerprint examinations "after two assistant public defenders raised serious concerns about its testing practices. A subsequent review by two independent consultants identified major flaws in nearly every aspect of the lab's operation, including dirty equipment, a lack of standard operating procedures, faulty testing techniques, illegible reports, and a woeful ignorance of basic scientific principles."

Months later, a former chemist of the Massachusetts drug laboratory in Boston "was indicted on 27 counts of obstructing justice, tampering with evidence, perjury and other charges in connection with her handling of some of the tens of thousands of drug cases she worked on during her nine years there. 'Little Annie' Dookhan is accused of faking test results, intentionally contaminating and padding suspected drug samples, forging co-workers' signatures on lab reports, and falsely claiming to have a master's degree in chemistry."

The 36-year-old Dookhan, the mother of a disabled child, pleaded guilty to 27 counts of misleading investigators, filing false reports, and tampering with evidence and, in November of 2013, was sentenced to three-to-five years in prison, according to The Boston Globe.

Early in 2013, Hansen reported, a review was under way by the New York City medical examiner's office of more than 800 rape cases from a 10-year period "during which DNA evidence may have been mishandled by a lab technician who resigned in 2011 after an internal review uncovered problems with her work." The review, Hansen wrote, "had already turned up 26 cases in which the former technician failed to detect the presence of DNA evidence, including one in which the evidence has since led to an arrest in a 10-year-old rape case. The review uncovered 19 cases in which DNA evidence was commingled with DNA evidence from other cases."

The possibility of tainted evidence is a recurring problem and long-standing criticism of DNA testing and analysis. In 2011, the Nassau

County, New York crime laboratory was shuttered following revelations of "serious problems with its drug analysis testing without informing anyone," Hansen wrote.

The problems at the lab included "improper maintenance of equipment and instruments, failure to properly mark and store evidence, and failure to secure the lab and adequately maintain records," according to the analysis.

***

More frightening than the specter of missing or accidentally tainted evidence, though, is the possibility of deliberate tampering with or falsification or withholding of evidence – as cited above and in a 2010 scandal involving the North Carolina State Bureau of Investigation's crime laboratory. Two retired FBI agents conducting an independent audit of that lab found that "analysts there had systematically withheld or distorted evidence in more than 230 cases over a 16-year period, including three cases that resulted in executions."

The audit, reported Hansen, was ordered following the exoneration of a man wrongly convicted in the 1991 murder of a prostitute. It found that "the lab's serology section had long had a policy of reporting that presumptive tests for the presence of blood were positive, while failing to reveal when confirmatory tests proved to be negative or inconclusive. As a matter of practice, analysts also filed reports that overstated their test results and contradicted their bench notes."

The Raleigh News & Observer investigated the scandal and found "overwhelming evidence of a pro-prosecution bias at the lab, including training materials advising analysts on how to improve their conviction rates and instructing them to be wary of defense experts, whom it referred to as 'defense whores,' " wrote Hansen. "Performance reviews were written by prosecutors praising individual analysts for their favorable testimony, and a video showed two blood-spatter experts congratulating each other when, after several failed attempts, they successfully recreated a scenario supporting the prosecution's theory of the case."

In 2009, the National Academy of Sciences released a study of forensic science that listed a number of problems in crime lab operations. The New York Times in its February 4 story previewing the study's findings and recommendations reported that "forensic evidence that has helped convict thousands of defendants for nearly a century is often the product of shoddy scientific practices that should be upgraded and standardized." The report, according to the Times, "says such analyses are often handled by poorly trained technicians who then exaggerate the accuracy of their methods in court," and "the field suffered from a reliance on outmoded and untested theories by analysts who often have no background in science, statistics or other empirical disciplines."

Other conclusions of the report, as summarized in Hansen's analysis, include:

> •"There is wide variability in forensic science disciplines, not only in techniques and methodologies but also in reliability, error rates, reporting, research, general acceptability and published material;

• "Many labs are underfunded and understaffed, which contributes to case backlogs and likely makes it more difficult for lab workers to do as much as they could to inform investigators, provide strong evidence for prosecutions and avoid errors"; and,

• "Most labs operate under the auspices of law enforcement agencies, making them susceptible to pressures – overt and otherwise – to produce the kinds of results that police and prosecutors are looking for."

In 2012, the American Bar Association House of Delegates adopted two resolutions at its midyear meeting, reported Hansen – both of which would have a bearing on future criminal proceedings involving the use of DNA forensics.

"One urges governments at all levels to adopt pretrial discovery procedures requiring crime labs to produce 'comprehensive and comprehensible' reports that spell out the procedure used in analysis; the results of the analysis; the identity, qualifications and opinions of the analyst and anybody else who participated in the testing; and any additional information that could bear on the validity of the test results. The other urges judges and lawyers to consider several factors in determining how expert testimony should be presented to a jury and in instructing juries how to evaluate that testimony."

***

Beyond the ethical and technical considerations, though, stands the overwhelming evidence of DNA testing and analysis successfully and legally employed to bring violent criminals to justice. The U.S. Supreme Court stamped its seal of approval on DNA testing in a major but narrow, 5-4, 2013 ruling enabling police to collect DNA from arrestees who have not been convicted of serious offenses. In his majority opinion, Justice Anthony M. Kennedy likened a DNA cheek swab to fingerprinting and photographs.

" 'An individual's identity is more than just his name or Social Security number, and the government's interest in identification goes beyond ensuring that the proper name is typed on the indictment,' " wrote Kennedy, as reported in the June 3, 2013 ABA Journal.

"Police take a mug shot and show it to witnesses; they take fingerprints and compare it to a database. 'In this respect the only difference between DNA analysis and the accepted use of fingerprint databases is the unparalleled accuracy DNA provides.' "

But Justice Antonin Scalia in his dissent worried about the broadening of such intrusion into privacy, which he saw as a violation of the Fourth Amendment's guarantee against unreasonable search and seizure. While the ruling would bring the benefit of solving more crimes, wrote Scalia, " 'so would the taking of DNA samples from anyone who flies on an airplane (surely the Transportation Security Administration needs to know the "identity" of the flying public), applies for a driver's license, or attends a public school. Perhaps the construction of such a genetic panopticon is wise. But I doubt that the proud men who wrote the charter of our liberties would have been so eager to open their mouths for royal inspection.' "

Nonetheless, wrote Kennedy, " 'the intrusion of a cheek swab to obtain a DNA sample is a minimal one' and is 'no different than matching an arrestee's face to a wanted poster of a previously unidentified suspect; or matching tattoos to known gang symbols to reveal a criminal affiliation; or matching the arrestee's fingerprints to those recovered from a crime scene.' "

In short, the legal judgment on behalf of the overall good trumps that of the civil libertarian's concern.

Statistical and anecdotal evidence of crimes solved through the use of DNA supports Kennedy's argument.

In June of 1997, serial rapist Lester Don Parks was linked, through the Texas CODIS system, to the July 1993 sexual assault of two sisters, aged 10 and 11, beneath a bridge in Granbury, Texas, 70 miles southwest of Dallas. Though police had semen samples, "there was little evidence to track him," wrote Katherine Ramsland in her 2004 book, "The Science of Cold Case Files," cited elsewhere in this book. "And there were no DNA databases in 1993, so without a suspect, there was no way to make use of the samples. Several other small towns reported similar incidents, but each case went cold."

But four years later, under the Texas CODIS program that required convicted sex offenders to submit blood samples for DNA profiles for the database, a detective submitted samples from the Granbury sisters and got a match to Parks, who lived a hundred miles east of Granbury. "The other similar cold cases hit on his name as well. He was a serial rapist. On June 5, 1999, he was convicted of indecency with a child."

Following are a few more examples of such evidence since the turn of this century.

In 2011, New York law enforcement officials charged a Rikers Island inmate with the 1986 killing of a 26-year-old woman who had been stabbed and strangled in a Harlem park. According to The New York Times' July 7 account of the case, it was "the first murder that a recently created Manhattan's district attorney's office cold case unit has solved through the use of new forensic techniques, prosecutors said." The 50-year-old Steven Carter was convicted on two counts of murder in June and sentenced to 25 years to life in prison.

A serial rapist/murderer was sentenced in December of 2003 in a Seattle court to 48 consecutive life terms after pleading guilty in November to 48 counts of first-degree murder.

Dubbed the "Green River Killer" because he had dumped his victims' bodies in the Green River in south King County, the 54-year-old truck driver "was arrested in November 2001 after detectives linked his DNA to sperm found in three of the earliest victims," reported the Associated Press on December 18, 2003. Gary Ridgway, who had targeted prostitutes, confessed that he "hated prostitutes and didn't want to pay them for sex, and that he killed so many women he had a hard time keeping them straight."

A 1979 slaying in New York, which had some similarities to the Janet Walsh case, was solved more than two decades later through analysis of DNA taken from a blood trail from a woman's Mount Vernon apartment. The evidence tied Walter Gill, a 49-year-old Sing Sing inmate doing time for nine felonies and eight misdemeanors, to the August 1979 stabbing death of Diane Gregory. Besides the young age of the victim, who was 22 after the year of the murder, and the year that the crime occurred, other similarities to the Walsh case included the discovery of both deceased women in their homes, DNA samples of the perpetrators had been left behind on bedding, and the evidence had been stored away for decades until DNA forensic technology arrived to help solve the cases. A relative in both cases – Gregory's sister and Walsh's father, Peter Caltury – played an active role in the investigative process. And each woman knew her killer.

"The investigation into Ms. Gregory's slaying was renewed this year after Carolyn Gregory, the dead woman's sister, asked a member of the Mount Vernon City Council if DNA might be used to glean fresh clues in the case," reported The New York Times on March 13, 2000. "The councilman approached the Mount Vernon Police Department, which then reviewed its files to see if old evidence existed.

"In this case, biological evidence abounded. Ms. Gregory's apartment had been splattered with blood, as had a pillowcase that had been pressed against her head, a piece of jagged glass and a sheet found at the end of the bloody trail that began at her body and continued outdoors and into the neighborhood.

"Some of this blood, detectives had long believed, came from her attacker.

"Moreover, a law enforcement official who is involved in the investigation said the Mount Vernon detectives' original case files indicated that Mr. Gill had known Ms. Gregory and had been a suspect from the beginning, but that investigators had lacked evidence powerful enough to file a charge or to get a court order to draw his blood for testing."

Newly enacted state legislation required Gill as an inmate to submit a sample of his DNA which, once entered into the statewide database, matched the DNA profile from the bed sheet, which also had traces of Gregory's blood. Once the sample was taken, Gill knew, Westchester District Attorney Jeanine F. Pirro told the Times for a story published the next day, "that he would be caught."

Gill confessed to the murder, Mount Vernon's then-police commissioner, Gertrude LaForgia, told the Times.

A different investigative technique was undertaken by Seattle police more than a decade ago to solve the rape-murder case of 13-year-old Kristen Sumstad, who had been found strangled in 1982, her body dumped in a cardboard box. Authorities suspected her former neighbor, then-14-year-old John Nicholas Athan who, on the night her body was found, "was seen pushing a hand truck carrying a large box. Under questioning, he claimed that he had been stealing firewood," wrote Ramsland.

"Police could not crack the case," Ramsland wrote, until more than 20 years later, when "they mailed Athan a document that involved a return envelope. Athan licked the envelope and sent it back, and the crime lab matched the DNA from his saliva to the semen sample taken from the victim. Athan's defense lawyer made a motion to have this evidence thrown out because it was gained through deception and by detectives who had illegally posed as attorneys. Athan's rights were violated," he said.

"But the prosecutor maintained that the police have often used such ruses to collect evidence. The judge ruled that the police did not break the law and therefore the DNA evidence was admissible and the defendant could stand trial. On January 21, 2004, Athan was convicted of second-degree murder."

Persistent efforts by law enforcement officials led to the closure in 2012 of a cold case when a DNA-assisted breakthrough ended a decade and a half of terror for a New York City woman who had been raped in her apartment in 1998.

"Fourteen years later, she has stopped sleeping with a knife under her pillow, but the pain is 'never ending,' a rape victim told a Manhattan judge today," reported the New York Post on October 23, 2012. " 'It seemed like the whole world had gone black and that the soundtrack to my life was the sound of sirens and screaming,' the victim of monster rapist Lerio Guerrero said in a letter read aloud as he was sentenced to 15 years in prison."

The symptoms reported by the rape victim in the letter mirror the angst and fears of other survivors of violent crimes, and of those who survive the victims of murder. The newspaper reported that the victim's "lingering flashbacks and terror cost her sleep, friends and her job," according to the letter.

" 'My life shrunk,' the woman – who was not present in the courtroom – said in a letter read into record by prosecutor Martha Bashford, who heads the Manhattan DA's sex crimes unit. 'I booby trapped my windows and door, and went to bed with a knife under my pillow; yet I rarely slept,' she wrote. She had since regained some of her former confidence, she wrote. Still, 'I will forever be haunted by that day.' "

That day occurred November 8, 1998, when the then-28-year-old college professor entered her Lower East Village apartment building and was pushed inside her apartment by then-20-year-old Guerrero, of Staten Island. Guerrero raped her and then robbed her.

"Not satisfied with just brutalizing her

and taking what was left in her wallet, the sicko dragged her to an ATM to steal her money," reported the New York Daily News on October 9, 2012. "He robbed her of $800, but as he forced her to a second ATM, the victim was able to break free and get help."

The victim's jacket had been spattered with Guerrero's blood after he'd cut himself on a glass shard, but the case then went cold. Years later, the office of New York District Attorney Cyrus R. Vance Jr. conducted a DNA analysis that led to Guerrero. The analysis was representative of the wide-ranging opportunities such examinations afford police investigators.

Chewing gum, soft drink cans, coffee cups – all offer potential DNA clues, it has been learned over the years. In Guerrero's case, it was a cigarette butt left behind at the scene of a 2011 rape that was under investigation, as recounted in a compelling story by The New York Times that detailed the rapid progress in DNA forensics.

"With the casual flick of a spent cigarette, Lerio Guerrero unwittingly demonstrated recent advances in DNA testing and a heretofore unspoken peril of smoking," the Times reported on June 15, 2011. The cigarette Guerrero had left behind at the scene of a sexual assault of a Brooklyn woman in May of 2011 – for which Guerrero was not charged – was given to the city's medical examiner's office, "where tests showed that his DNA matched the rape kit and blood evidence from a different crime: the rape of a woman on the Lower East Side in 1998," according to Vance, the Times reported.

"The developments in the cases underscored efforts by Mr. Vance to exploit the science of DNA testing. He has been educating his staff on the uses of DNA and has assigned a team to reexamine unsolved murders and sex crimes from years past to see if DNA evidence can help crack the cold cases.

"So far, his office has secured 57 John Doe indictments, most of them in rape cases. As of March 10, 14 of them had been arrested, said Erin Duggan, the chief spokeswoman for Mr. Vance's office.

"Vance", the story continued, was trying to amend state laws to broaden collection of biological evidence. And in his jurisdiction, Vance and his predecessor, Robert M. Morgenthau, were increasing their focus on the use of such forensics.

"He has set up a Forensic Sciences Cold Case Unit, whose mission is to train prosecutors to expand the use of DNA evidence to include assaults and property crimes; to re-energize efforts to solve unsolved homicides from decades ago; and to push for the new state law to broaden the state's DNA databank to include all types of crimes," reported the newspaper.

Vance's efforts were similar to nationwide initiatives.

"Around the country," the newspaper reported, "police departments and prosecutors have become increasingly reliant on DNA technology, seeking to detect the presence of DNA on evidence and figuring out ways to use it in criminal trials, several analysts said. Some have praised Mr. Vance's efforts but also warned of the dangers of blindly accepting DNA findings, and some questioned whether tight municipal budgets or a lack of qualified personnel might undercut his efforts."

It is a continuing story.

Steve Hallock is director of graduate studies for
the School of Communication at Pittsburgh's Point
Park University. A former newspaper writer and
editor, he is the author of four previous books. He
has published commentaries on op-ed pages that
include The New York Times, Pittsburgh Post-
Gazette, Philadelphia Inquirer, St. Louis Post-
Dispatch and Denver Post, and fiction in literary
journals. He lives with his wife, Joanne, in Mt.
Lebanon, a suburb of Pittsburgh, PA.

CPSIA information can be obtained at www.ICGtesting.com
Printed in the USA
BVOW04s0612071015

421346BV00010B/255/P

9 780996 459204